Presented to:

____

Presented by:

____

Walking the Chosen Path: Godly Wisdom to Direct Your Steps

Published by J. Countryman®, a division of Thomas Nelson, Inc., Nashville, Tennessee 37214

Project Editor: Alice Sullivan
Writing and Compilation: SnapdragonGroupSM Editorial Services, Tulsa, Oklahoma.
Design: Thinkpen Design, llc

ISBN: 1-404-18662-X

Printed and bound in the United States of America
www.thomasnelson.com | www.jcountryman.com

WALKING THE CHOSEN PATH

GODLY WISDOM TO DIRECT YOUR STEPS

A Division of Thomas Nelson Publishers
Since 1798
www.thomasnelson.com

Introduction

God has given each person the gift of a free and sovereign will. In other words, we have the right to choose for ourselves the path we will take in life. And yet, because He loves us dearly, He stands with hand outstretched, softly urging, "Choose Me, follow Me." His promise is that when we do, He will gently lead us through the maze of available options to the ones that will bring us love, joy, peace, and fulfillment.

Walking the Chosen Path was written to encourage you to look to Him, your Creator, the one who has always loved you, as you face those crucial choices in your life. Take His hand, listen for His voice, read His Word, share the longings of your heart with Him in prayer. God is near. He is waiting, listening, urging you to choose the path that leads to life, both now and for eternity.

One person who has mastered life is better than a thousand persons who have mastered only the contents of books. But no one can get anything out of life without God.

Meister Eckhart
(1260-1327)
Dominican Preacher and Theologian

Acceptance

"Man looks at the outward appearance,
but the LORD looks at the heart."
1 SAMUEL 16:7 NKJV

If God accepts me as I am,
then I had better do the same.
HUGH MONTEFIORE

In Christ, there is no difference between Jew and Greek,
slave and free person, male and female. You are all
the same in Christ Jesus. You belong to Christ.
GALATIANS 3:28–29 NCV

God Accepts Everyone!

He chose us in Him before the foundation of the world ... according to the good pleasure of His will, to the praise of the glory of His grace, by which He made us accepted in the Beloved.

EPHESIANS 1:4–6 NKJV

God accepts you—faults and all. Can you do the same for those around you? It's easy to get off track. A different race, different religious beliefs, even a different style of clothes can lead you to make judgments before you even carry on a conversation with someone.

The key is to bypass what you see and focus on what you know. God created each person with great love and care. God accepts each person, even if he or she has not accepted Him. The more you learn to view others through God's love, instead of sizing them up with your eyes, the easier it will be to accept them as equals, treat them as friends, and love them as God's precious children.

Heavenly Father,

Thank You that You accept me just the way I am, no matter what. I want to be as accepting of others as You have been of me. Help me to see other people through Your loving eyes and accept them as my brothers and sisters in You.

Amen.

Approval

What must our natures be like before [God] can feel at home within us? He asks nothing but a pure heart and a single mind. He desires but sincerity, transparency, humility, and love.

A. W. TOZER

The kingdom of God is not eating and drinking, but righteousness and peace and joy in the Holy Spirit. For he who serves Christ in these things is acceptable to God.

ROMANS 14:17–18 NKJV

Little self-denials, little honesties, little passing words of sympathy, little nameless acts of kindness, little silent victories over favorite temptations—these are the silent threads of gold which, when woven together, gleam out so brightly in the pattern of life that God approves.

FREDERIC WILLIAM FARRAR

Losing Your Performance Anxiety

Be diligent to present yourself approved to God,
a worker who does not need to be ashamed,
rightly dividing the word of truth.
2 TIMOTHY 2:15 NKJV

Most people suffer from chronic performance anxiety. Is that the case with you? Are you constantly wondering what kind of reviews you will receive from your family, your boss, your friends, or your coworkers? If so, here's a little stage wisdom to help you cope.

Kill the foot lights and turn up the house lights. When you do, you will see that there is only one VIP in the audience—God. Ultimately, His review is the only one that matters. When you live your life in a manner that is pleasing to Him, it will build your confidence because it will be established on something solid, instead of on the shifting sands of people's opinions. So, chase away your anxiety and live your life for God. You're bound to be a hit with Him.

Heavenly Father,

You are the audience member who really counts. Help me to live a life that is pleasing to You and to look only for Your approval, not for the approval of those around me. I want to receive a standing ovation from You.

Amen.

Assurance

God our Savior ... wants all people to be saved
and to know the truth. There is one God
and one way human beings can reach God.
That way is through Christ Jesus.

1 TIMOTHY 2:3–5 NCV

The assurance of salvation is one
of God's beautiful gifts. Every believer
ought to know that he possesses salvation.

GEORGE SWEETING

[Jesus said,] "Most assuredly, I say to you,
he who hears My word and believes in Him who sent Me
has everlasting life, and shall not come into judgment,
but has passed from death into life."

JOHN 5:24 NKJV

Sure of Where You're Headed

Whoever calls on the name
of the LORD Shall be saved.
ACTS 2:21 NKJV

Some people believe that you can't be certain of your salvation until after you die. But the New Testament is filled with assurances—that God's deep desire is for everyone to receive the gift of salvation, that Christ's sacrifice on the cross was sufficient to cover all sin, that any person who is forgiven and cleansed by Christ's blood is heir to eternal life.

God doesn't want you to live your life wondering if you will make it to Heaven. He wants you to know that He is preparing a place for you. Jesus said to the thief who hung beside Him on the cross, "This day you will be with me in paradise." That day, with his dying breath, a criminal turned to Jesus and received the assurance of his salvation.

Heavenly Father,

I thank You so much for the assurance of my salvation. I don't have to spend my life wondering what will happen to me when I die. I know that I have a heavenly home awaiting me because I have been forgiven of my sins and given a new life in You.

Amen.

Belief

Without faith no one can please God. Anyone who comes to God must believe that he is real and that he rewards those who truly want to find him.

HEBREWS 11:6 NCV

The point of having an open mind, like having an open mouth, is to close it on something solid.

G. K. CHESTERTON

You have not seen Christ, but still you love him. You cannot see him now, but you believe in him. So you are filled with a joy that cannot be explained, a joy full of glory.

1 PETER 1:8 NCV

Anything Is Possible!

Jesus said ..., "If you can believe,
all things are possible to him who believes."
MARK 9:23 NKJV

As a kid, you probably believed some unbelievable things, like the tooth fairy exchanged molars for cash or that Santa shimmied down your chimney on Christmas Eve. What you believed, true or not, influenced your actions. You put your tooth under your pillow and left cookies out for Santa.

Some aspects of God seem unbelievable. But, He's no fairy tale. Put the historicity of Jesus and the faithfulness of God's promises to the test. Know what you believe and why.

Then, don't just say you believe in God; act on that belief. Release guilt and regret, believing God's forgiven you. Risk being authentically you, believing God created you for a unique purpose. Reach out to others, believing love is God's highest aim for your life.

Heavenly Father,

I want to believe in You. Help my unbelief, Lord. Help me to have the faith that I need and then to act on that faith, no matter what the circumstances of my life might try to tell me. Anything is possible as I place my trust in You and live out my faith through my actions.

Amen.

Blessings

Reflect upon your present blessings,
of which every man has many, not on your past
misfortunes, of which all men have some.

CHARLES DICKENS

Those who are called by God can
now receive the blessings he has promised,
blessings that will last forever.

HEBREWS 9:15 NCV

The more we count the blessings
we have, the less we crave the luxuries we haven't.

WILLIAM ARTHUR WARD

Blessed with Every Blessing

Praise be to the God and Father of our Lord Jesus Christ. In Christ, God has given us every spiritual blessing in the heavenly world.

EPHESIANS 1:3 NCV

When you think about counting your blessings, your mind most likely turns to those you can see—a warm place to live, food in the fridge, friends and family to hold you close. But, the blessings that God showers on you every day go far beyond what you can touch with your hands.

God's blessings include miracles like the process of prayer, a future home in heaven, and God's ultimate gift of salvation. Although blessings like these are really more than the human mind can understand, they are also easily taken for granted. Take time right now to send God a heartfelt thank-you note via prayer. Ask Him to help your gratitude grow by making you increasingly more aware of every blessing He brings your way.

Heavenly Father,

Thank You for all of the blessings that You pour out upon my life every day—both the obvious blessings that I can see and touch with my hands and the less obvious ones, the many spiritual blessings I have in Christ. Help my gratitude to grow as I count my blessings each day.

Amen.

Career

No life can be dreary when work is delight.

FRANCES RIDLEY HAVERGAL

God has made us what we are. In Christ Jesus, God made us to do good works, which God planned in advance for us to live our lives doing.

EPHESIANS 2:10 NCV

Our forefathers succeeded
because their goal was not material
wealth alone but glory to God.
...They believed whatever
they did was God ordained.

TOM HAGGAI

Finding Your Life's Work

Each person has his own gift from God.
One has one gift, another has another gift.
1 CORINTHIANS 7:7 NCV

A career is defined as a profession or vocation. It's more than just a job. Your career is your life's work. It should be something you love, something you feel you were born to do. Sounds simple—but it isn't always so easy to put your finger on. If you feel that way, you aren't alone. Many people stop and start a few times before they find their truest calling.

No matter what, don't settle for less. Keep looking and trying new things until you find the proper career path for you. You'll know it by the little leap your heart takes when you think and pray about it. You'll know because God will confirm it to you deep inside. Life is too short to spend it doing anything but what God has called you to do.

Heavenly Father,

I don't want to settle for anything less than what You have called me to do. Help me to find the right career path that will tap into my specific gifts and talents. As I step out into the world, guide my steps—and my heart—and let me know when I have found what You have created me to do.

Amen.

Character

The LORD sees everything you do,
and he watches where you go.
PROVERBS 5:21 NCV

Character is what you are in the dark.
DWIGHT L. MOODY

Keep your eyes focused on what is right,
and look straight ahead to what is good.
Be careful what you do,
and always do what is right.
PROVERBS 4:25–26 NCV

Who Are You When Nobody's Watching?

We show we are servants of God by our pure lives.

2 CORINTHIANS 6:6 NCV

Your character is who you are when no one's watching. It's the very best of you, and worst of you, all rolled into one. One of the goals of maturing is to get your character in line with who God created you to be.

Though there is no one quite like you, there are qualities your character should share with all those who follow God. Traits such as honesty, integrity, generosity, and deep-hearted love should be an essential part of who you are and how you relate in this life as God's child.

But, character develops out of choice, not chance. Choose to work on erasing any traits that don't reflect God's own character. Ask for God's help in developing the qualities most like His own.

Heavenly Father,

I want my character to be in line with Your character, with the character of those who follow You in their daily lives. Help me to choose to develop my character by making the daily decision to become more like You. As I live out Your love in this life, I will be a godly man or woman of God—no matter who's watching or not.

Amen.

Church

The church is filled with Christ, and Christ fills everything in every way.

EPHESIANS 1:23 NCV

Church-goers are like coals in a fire. When they cling together, they keep the flame aglow; when they separate, they die out.

BILLY GRAHAM

As we have many members in one body, but all the members do not have the same function, so we, being many, are one body in Christ, and individually members of one another.

ROMANS 12:4–5 NKJV

Finding Your Place in the Family of God

You should not stay away from the church meetings,
as some are doing, but you should meet
together and encourage each other.
HEBREWS 10:25 NCV

There's a church out there that needs you. It isn't complete without you. What awaits is a support group of friends, opportunities to use the gifts God's given you, and an environment where you can grow. But, you have to make the first move.

If your life has taken you in a new direction, don't put off finding a church you can call home. If you're already part of a church, check your involvement level. If you're over- or under-involved, ask God to help you find a healthy balance. Then, use your newfound freedom to make a wise choice to follow His leading. Honor God and feed your own hungry soul by attending a weekly service. Go with a teachable mind and a servant's heart—and enjoy.

Heavenly Father,

You have said that Your people should not forsake the assembling of ourselves together. I don't want to be a "lone ranger" when it comes to Your Church—I want to be a fully involved, active participant. Help me to find my place in Your family, a place where I can use my spiritual gifts to serve You better.

Amen.

Comfort

In Christ the heart of the Father is revealed,
the higher comfort there cannot be
than to rest in the Father's heart.

ANDREW MURRAY

The LORD will hear your crying,
and he will comfort you.
When he hears you, he will help you.

ISAIAH 30:19 NCV

God does not comfort us to make us comfortable,
but to make us comforters.

HENRY JOWETT

God Is Near

The LORD wants to show his mercy to you.
He wants to rise and comfort you.
The LORD is a fair God,
and everyone who waits for his help will be happy.

ISAIAH 30:18 NCV

Everyone weeps. Even if your tears are not visible to those around you, life on this imperfect earth is bound to break your heart now and then. But, you have a Father who loves you deeply. He doesn't want your heart to remain in shattered pieces. Like a mother who runs to her child's side the moment she hears a pain-filled cry, God is near, offering tender comfort when you need it most.

When your heart is crying out for healing, cry out to God. He'll never put you down for being overly emotional or tell you to grow up. Instead, He'll go to the source of your heartbreak, soothing your soul with peace and perspective. Allow God to dry your tears with His love.

Heavenly Father,

You have not left me comfortless, but You have promised to be with me no matter what happens. When I need Your comfort the most, help me to reach out to You. Place Your loving arms around me and dry my tears with Your gracious love.

Amen.

Commitment

Those who are innocent and who do what is right ...
keep their promises to their neighbors, even when it hurts.

PSALM 15:2, 4 NCV

The moment one definitely commits oneself,
the Providence moves too. All sorts of things occur
to help that would never otherwise have occurred.

W. H. MURRAY

If you make a promise to God, don't be slow
to keep it. God is not happy with fools,
so give God what you promised.

ECCLESIASTES 5:4 NCV

Keeping Your Word

If a man makes a promise to the LORD or says he will do something special, he must keep his promise. He must do what he said.

NUMBERS 30:2 NCV

God is committed to you. He won't bail on His promises or put you on "prayer waiting" because a more important call has come in. He will do what He says.

Before you make a commitment, whether to a relationship, a job, or even to volunteer to sell donuts at church on Sunday mornings, you need to weigh the cost. Ask yourself if your time, energy, resources, and talents are all at a level where you can follow through on your promise. Ask God to help you only make commitments that fit with His purpose and direction for your life.

Then, make one more commitment. Commit whatever you're doing to God. Through success, failure, struggles, and growth, allow Him to help you keep your word.

Heavenly Father,

I want to be the kind of person who can be counted on to keep my word. When I make a commitment, help me first count the cost and then follow through on what I have said I will do. In this way, I will be a better representation of You to others. I place all of my commitments in Your hands.

Amen.

Compassion

Man is never nearer the Divine than
in his compassionate moments.

JOSEPH H. HERTZ

All of you be of one mind, having compassion for one another; love as brothers, be tenderhearted, be courteous; not returning evil for evil or reviling for reviling, but on the contrary blessing, knowing that you were called to this, that you may inherit a blessing.

1 PETER 3:8–9 NKJV

Man may dismiss compassion
from his heart, but God will never.

WILLIAM COWPER

Seeing the World through God's Eyes

You, O Lord, are a God full of compassion, and gracious,
Longsuffering and abundant in mercy and truth.

PSALM 86:15 NKJV

Imagine what it would be like to see the world through God's eyes. How would you feel about the woman in the wheelchair at the grocery store? The neighbor kid who's just found out his folks are getting a divorce? The homeless guy on the park bench?

Seeing individuals the way God does makes you want to put love into action and help. That's compassion kicking in. Compassion doesn't just feel sorry for people, though. It strives to make a positive difference in their lives. So, ask God to help you see through His eyes—then to let you know how to help. Even if the only action you can take is to pray, your compassion can make a difference in the world.

Heavenly Father,

You see the world through eyes of compassion, and You care for everyone as if they were the only person in the entire world. I want to have that kind of compassion in my life. Help me to see people through Your eyes of love and take actions that will make a difference in my world.

Amen.

Confidence

Nothing can be done without hope and confidence.
HELEN ADAMS KELLER

It is better to trust in the LORD
Than to put confidence in man.
PSALM 118:8 NKJV

Our confidence in Christ ... awakens us,
urges us on, and makes us active in living
righteous lives and doing good.
There is no self-confidence to compare with this.
ULRICH ZWINGLI

Self-assurance or God-assurance?

The LORD will be your confidence,
And will keep your foot from being caught.
PROVERBS 3:26 NKJV

The first rule of any job interview is to act confident. But, where does that confidence come from? Is it found in your education? Your natural abilities? Your family connections? The new designer suit you happen to be wearing?

Confidence in anything other than God's love for you and His power working through you is not sturdy enough to build an accurate self-image on. Self-assurance is great, but God-assurance is what's going to keep you going through the ups and downs of life.

When you're faced with a challenge, thank God for the strengths and assets He's provided you with. Then, refuse to rely solely on them. Firmly place your confidence on God—on who He is and who He says you are in Him.

Heavenly Father,

Thank You for the many gifts and talents You have placed within me. I know that You have given me many skills in which I can have confidence, but my real confidence must always lie in my relationship with You—in who Your Word says that I am. Thank You that I can always find my confidence in You.

Amen.

Contentment

God is most glorified in us when
we are most satisfied in him.

JOHN PIPER

I say it is better to be content
with what little you have.
Otherwise, you will always be struggling for more,
and that is like chasing the wind.

ECCLESIASTES 4:6 NCV

The secret of contentment is the
realization that life is a gift, not a right.

AUTHOR UNKNOWN

Letting Go of the "If Onlys"

I have learned in whatever state I am, to be content.
PHILIPPIANS 4:11 NKJV

How much is enough? To a contented heart, it's as much as God has chosen to provide. To measure your personal level of contentment, complete this sentence: I would be content if only....

What are the "if onlys" in your life? More money? Being involved in a serious relationship? Losing or gaining weight? Landing the job of your dreams?

There's another name for "if onlys." They're called idols. When your desires move from "it would be nice" to "I can't be happy without," you've chosen to believe some thing can satisfy you, instead of Someone. Ask God to reveal any "if onlys" you need to confront. Then, ask Him to show you how to find contentment where you are and with what you have right now.

Heavenly Father,

You are the true satisfaction of my life. I let go of any "if onlys" I have been holding on to and instead look to You to bring true contentment to my soul. I know that the things of this earth won't truly satisfy me—but I can find real contentment right now in my relationship with You.

Amen.

Courage

Be strong and of good courage; do not be afraid,
nor be dismayed, for the LORD your God
is with you wherever you go.

JOSHUA 1:9 NKJV

Courage is fear that has said its prayers.

DOROTHY BERNARD

Wait on the LORD;
Be of good courage,
And He shall strengthen your heart.

PSALM 27:14 NKJV

Standing Up to the Giants

Don't lose your courage or be afraid. Don't panic or be frightened, because the LORD your God goes with you, to fight for you against your enemies and to save you.

DEUTERONOMY 20:3–4 NCV

It takes courage to go where God leads. He'll often take you right to the doorstep of your greatest fears, put you face-to-face with someone you can't stand to be around, or bring a situation into your life that seems impossible to work out. Don't panic. Those are the times when you can really see God's power in action.

You were never created to handle tough times alone. Consider David. The only reason he could conquer a giant was because God was with him. You have the same advantage. God is fighting every battle with you, never against you.

So, take courage. Stand up to the giants in your life. With God's help, victory is at hand.

Heavenly Father,

Many situations in life seem to be difficult to handle, but I know that because You are with me, I can have the courage to face anything that comes my way. I commit to stand up to the giants in my life, with Your gracious help.

Amen.

Decisions

We make our decisions, and then our decisions turn around and make us.

FRANCIS BOREHAM

A man's heart plans his way,
But the LORD directs his steps.

PROVERBS 16:9 NKJV

God always gives his very best to those who leave the choice with him.

JAMES HUDSON TAYLOR

ASKING FOR GOD'S ADVICE

You guide me with your advice,
and later you will receive me in honor.
PSALM 73:24 NCV

When you're faced with a tough decision, it's only natural to go to a friend for advice. Chatting openly with someone who knows you and your situation well can help you put the pros and cons of your options into clearer perspective. So, what could make more sense than spending time talking things over with the One who knows you better than anyone else?

God cares about the direction in which your life is headed. The decisions you make each day help determine that direction. Weighing your decisions by what's written in the Bible and using the wisdom that God provides for the asking will not only help you determine right from wrong, but better from best.

Heavenly Father,

The Bible tells me that when I need wisdom, all I need to do is ask, and You will gladly help me know which decision to make. Thank You for Your care for my life and that You love me more than anyone else does. I am determined to make my choices according to Your Word and with the wisdom that comes only from You.

Amen.

Determination

The difference between the impossible
and the possible lies in a man's determination.
TOMMY LASORDA

*We have troubles all around us, but
we are not defeated. We do not know what to do,
but we do not give up the hope of living.*
2 CORINTHIANS 4:8 NCV

I've always made a total effort, even when the odds
seemed entirely against me. I never quit trying;
I never felt that I didn't have a chance to win.
ARNOLD PALMER

Don't Give Up!

*Do not cast away your confidence, which has great reward.
For you have need of endurance, so that after you have
done the will of God, you may receive the promise.*
HEBREWS 10:35–36 NKJV

Have you ever wondered if life is worth the trouble? After all, it seems to be filled with heartache and disappointment and frustration. Sometimes, it's just plain boring and exhausting. God understands that you will sometimes feel like giving up. But He wants you to keep on going, refusing to quit until you have fulfilled the purpose for which He created you. That is determination.

God knows that every day of your life is important and worth living. One day there will be sweet rest. But for now, God is urging you to set your course and determine to see it through. And you should know that He is even more determined than you could ever be to see you finish the race He's set fore you.

Heavenly Father,

I choose this day to never give up. I am determined to live my life in a way that is pleasing to You, to persevere through all of the trouble, heartache, disappointment, and frustration, because I know that in the end, the prize that You have waiting for me will be worth it all. I will finish the race!

Amen.

Doubt

God has never turned away
the questions of a sincere searcher.

MAX L. LUCADO

Jesus said, "Do not be afraid; only believe."

MARK 5:36 NKJV

It need not discourage us if we are full of doubts. Healthy questions keep faith dynamic. Unless we start with doubts we cannot have a deep-rooted faith. One who believes lightly and unthinkingly has not much of a belief. He who has a faith which is not to be shaken has won it through blood and tears—has worked his way from doubt to truth as one who reaches a clearing through a thicket of brambles and thorns.

HELEN ADAMS KELLER

Standing in Belief

Jesus said to Thomas, "Reach your finger here,
and look at My hands; and reach your hand here, and
put it into My side. Do not be unbelieving, but believing."
JOHN 20:27 NKJV

Belief is not the absence of doubt, but the decision to stand in the midst of your doubts. Thomas had his doubts when the other disciples told him that Jesus had risen from the dead. But when Jesus appeared, He never condemned Thomas. Instead, He gave him evidence. He simply encouraged Thomas to touch Him and believe.

God doesn't condemn you for your doubts either. He just wants you to reach out to Him, to let Him prove to you that He does indeed exist. He desires to win you with His love and draw you to Him with His kindness. Bring your doubts to Jesus; lay them at His feet in prayer. Let Him turn your doubts to belief.

Heavenly Father,

I know that on this side of heaven not all of my doubts will be resolved. But I choose to stand in faith despite those doubts; I choose to take You at Your Word. Lord, I believe; help my unbelief. I cast my doubts at Your feet and ask You to give me the faith I need to really believe.

Amen.

Encouragement

Encouragement is oxygen to the soul.

GEORGE M. ADAMS

Encourage each other every day while it is "today."

HEBREWS 3:13 NCV

One of the highest of human duties
is the duty of encouragement.

WILLIAM BARCLAY

Being an Encourager

May our Lord Jesus Christ himself and God our Father encourage you and strengthen you in every good thing you do and say.

2 THESSALONIANS 2:16–17 NCV

Encouragement is more than building others up with your words. It's helping them find the courage to move ahead in a positive direction.

When God opens your eyes to someone who's discouraged, disappointed, or in need of comfort, ask Him for the wisdom to know the best words and actions to share. Then, let God's love for you encourage your own heart so that you can reach out in confidence, kindness, and humility.

Whatever you do or say, remember that it's God's love and power working through you that ultimately help another person—not your own superior counseling abilities. When God uses you in the lives of others, always thank Him for the privilege of being an encourager.

Heavenly Father,

I have been encouraged so that I might be an encouragement to other people. Use me to help the people You place in my life. Place Your words in my mouth so that the things I say will bring encouragement to others. I want to be Your hands and feet to those who need Your love.

Amen.

Eternal Life

Live near to God, and all things will appear little to you in comparison with eternal realities.

ROBERT MURRAY MCCHEYNE

Those who believe in the Son have eternal life.

JOHN 3:36 NCV

I thank thee, O Lord, that thou hast so set eternity within my heart that no earthly thing can ever satisfy me wholly.

JOHN BAILLIE

Never Lose Sight of Eternity

Jesus said, "This is eternal life: that people know you, the only true God, and that they know Jesus Christ, the One you sent."

JOHN 17:3 NCV

Your life will not end with a death certificate. God has made that null and void. There's true life ahead, at a deeper and more beautiful level than anything you can possibly experience in this world broken by sin.

Life on Earth is really just the beginning. It's like the childhood of your eternity. Today's your chance to grow and learn, to get acquainted with God and His creations, to get a small, inviting taste of what's to come.

Take hold of today with your whole heart. Enjoy it. Explore it. Give yourself fully toward living it well. But, never lose sight of eternity. There's so much more to living and real life than what you can see from where you stand right now.

Heavenly Father,

Thank You for Your free gift of eternal life. I know that this life is not all there is, that there is a greater life that awaits me in the future. Help me to grow in You and experience all I need to learn in this life to prepare me for the next.

Amen.

Expectancy

High expectations are the key to everything.

SAM WALTON

The eyes of all look expectantly to You. ...
You open Your hand
And satisfy the desire of every living thing.

PSALM 145:15–16 NKJV

There is something new every day if you look for it.

HANNAH HURNARD

YOUR BEST LIFE IS YET TO COME!

With God's power working in us, God can do much, much more than anything we can ask or imagine.

EPHESIANS 3:20 NCV

You've been waiting for months for the release of the sequel to your favorite movie. Finally, the time has come. You've waited in line, purchased your ticket, and found yourself a seat. You have an idea of what lies ahead, but you don't know exactly what's going to happen. All you know is that it's bound to be great.

That's the kind of expectation you can have about the life God has planned for you. He is more creative than any filmmaker, more amazing than any special effects, and more wonderful than any cinematic hero. You may not fully understand your story's beauty until you've reached the finale, but God promises that every detail of the plot has been chosen for your ultimate good.

Heavenly Father,

You are the best of what's yet to be! Thank You that my life is in Your hands and that You have amazing plans for me, plans that I cannot even imagine. As I trust in You and let Your power work through me, great things will happen!

Amen.

Faith

Faith is an activity; it is something that has to be applied.

CORRIE TEN BOOM

Faith means being sure of the things we hope for and knowing that something is real even if we do not see it. ... It was by faith that Noah heard God's warnings about things he could not yet see. He obeyed God and built a large boat to save his family. ... It was by faith Abraham obeyed God's call to go to another place God promised to give him. He left his own country, not knowing where he was to go.

HEBREWS 11:1, 7–8 NCV

Faith is the bird that sings when the dawn is still dark.

SIR RABINDRANATH TAGORE

Taking Action on What You Believe

My brothers and sisters, if people say they have faith, but do nothing, their faith is worth nothing.

JAMES 2:14 NCV

Faith is trust that's put to the test. It acts on what it believes to be true. If you have faith that your best friend can keep a secret, you'll risk being honest about your biggest mistakes and regrets. If you have faith that God really loves you, you'll risk making a decision you believe will honor Him, even if it promises not to be easy.

Faith grows the more you use it, the more you try it on for size. Give God the chance to grow yours. Act on what He's asked you to do. Risk moving out of your comfort level. Do more than believe with your heart. Move forward in faith, wherever He's leading you to go.

Heavenly Father,

I want to live a life that is characterized by a vibrant, growing faith. I want my faith to be put into action. Help me to take risks that are based on my faith, and cause the faith I have to grow more and more as I trust in You.

Amen.

Faithfulness

A faithful witness does not lie.

PROVERBS 14:5 NKJV

Faithfulness in little things is a big thing.

SAINT JOHN CHRYSOSTOM

A faithful man will abound with blessings.

PROVERBS 28:20 NKJV

Walking in God's Footsteps

My eyes shall be on the faithful of the land,
That they may dwell with me;
He who walks in a perfect way,
He shall serve me.

PSALM 101:6 NKJV

God will never waver in His faithfulness toward you. But, faithfulness is not a quality reserved for deity. With God's help, you can be faithful in your relationships with others, as well as with Him.

Just look to Him as your example. Ask yourself, "How would God treat this person?" or "What decision would most likely make God smile?" Whatever your answer, it involves some aspect of God's faithfulness.

When your promises can be trusted, your commitments can be depended upon, and your friends know they can rely on you to be devoted and true, you're faithfully walking in God's own footsteps.

Heavenly Father,

You have always been faithful to me and never let me down. You keep every promise in Your Word and You can be counted on, no matter what, to do what You say You will do. Help me to walk in Your footsteps of faithfulness. I want to be someone who can be depended on to keep my word. When I meet You face-to-face, I want to hear You say, "Well done, good and faithful servant."

Amen.

Family

The family is an everlasting anchorage, a quiet harbor.

RICHARD BYRD

The father of a good child is very happy;
parents who have wise children are glad because of them.
Make your father and mother happy;
give your mother a reason to be glad.

PROVERBS 23:24–25 NCV

Loving relationships are a family's best protection against the challenges of the world.

BERNIE WIEBE

Honor Your Father and Mother

The command says, "Honor your father and mother"
This is the first command that has a promise with it—
"Then everything will be well with you, and you
will have a long life on the earth."
EPHESIANS 6:2–3 NCV

For many young adults, family relationships change when life at home draws to a close. The change from living with your folks to being on your own is an exciting one. But, your address isn't the only thing that undergoes a transition. So does your relationship with your family. As always, God provides guidelines on handling the relational challenges ahead.

No matter what your age, God asks that you honor your parents. Period. He doesn't add "if they deserve it" or "until you leave home." Honor is to be a lifelong gift from you to your parents.

No matter what your family background, God can guide you through every season of your life in a way that honors the parents God gave you.

Heavenly Father,

As my relationship with my parents and family begins to change, help me to continue to honor my mother and father as You have asked me to. Even though life may be taking some exciting turns, thank You that the love of a family never changes.

Amen.

Fellowship

Do not be interested only in your own life,
but be interested in the lives of others.

PHILIPPIANS 2:4 NCV

No man is an island, entire of itself;
every man is a piece of the
continent, a part of the main.

JOHN DONNE

All of you should be in agreement,
understanding each other, loving each
other as family, being kind and humble.

1 PETER 3:8 NCV

A Common Bond

If we live in the light, as God is in the light,
we can share fellowship with each other.
1 JOHN 1:7 NCV

Fellowship is an old-fashioned-sounding word, bringing to mind potlucks—complete with fat-laden casseroles and colorful gelatin salads—eaten in church basement fellowship halls. But, true fellowship is never out of date. It's people living on the cutting edge of community, sharing life together.

When Christ is the center of that life, that common bond is more than friendship. It's a love that matures through differences and struggle, as well as through praise and play.

To experience fellowship, you have to involve your life with the lives of other people who believe in Christ. You need to risk being real and work your way through problems, instead of running from them. Only then can you experience the joy that being part of God's family brings.

Heavenly Father,

Thank You for true fellowship that is centered on You and Your family. That kind of fellowship endures and matures, no matter what circumstances life may bring. Help me to continue to involve my life with the lives of Your people, and receive the joy that such fellowship brings.

Amen.

Finances

Honor the LORD with your wealth and the firstfruits from all your crops. Then your barns will be full, and your wine barrels will overflow with new wine.

PROVERBS 3:9–10 NCV

If a person gets his attitude toward money straight, it will help straighten out almost every other area in his life.

BILLY GRAHAM

[Jesus said,] "Whoever can be trusted with a little can also be trusted with a lot, and whoever is dishonest with a little is dishonest with a lot."

LUKE 16:10 NCV

A Truly Rich Life

Jesus said to them, "Be careful and guard against all kinds of greed. Life is not measured by how much one owns."

LUKE 12:15 NCV

As the proud owner of a diploma, the promise of financial freedom lies ahead. Budgets, taxes, and bottom lines will be more a part of your life than ever before. The challenge is to prevent what you own from owning you.

A rich life is not measured in paychecks or possessions. It's measured by the depth of your relationship with God and others. Handling money wisely by spending within your budget, using credit cautiously, saving for the future, and giving generously as God's Word directs will help you keep money in perspective. It's just a tool, not a true treasure. Ask God to help you spend what you have, no matter how much or little that is, in a way that honors Him.

Heavenly Father,

I want the kind of rich life that only surrender to Your will can bring. Help me to keep my finances in order, to manage money wisely, and to keep all things in perspective. I want to always honor You with the resources You have provided for me.

Amen.

Forgiveness

Forgiveness is the key that unlocks the door
of resentment and the handcuffs of hate.
It is a power that breaks the chains of bitterness
and the shackles of selfishness.

CORRIE TEN BOOM

"You shall not take vengeance, nor bear any grudge against the children of your people, but you shall love your neighbor as yourself: I am the LORD."

LEVITICUS 19:18 NKJV

When you forgive, you in no way change the past—
but you sure do change the future.

BERNARD MELTZER

Lay Down the Weight

Forgive each other just as God forgave you in Christ.
EPHESIANS 4:32 NCV

A grudge is a heavy weight to carry. It can consume your thoughts, infect your attitude, and even adversely affect your health. You can't get rid of it by simply trying to forget you've been hurt. You have to replace it with something that heals the pain. That "something" is forgiveness.

Forgiving someone doesn't excuse what happened or automatically mend a relationship. It doesn't mean you're "weak" for giving in. It means you're strong enough to willingly choose to imitate God's character. It means you're courageous enough to practice real love in an often unloving world.

That's something that requires God's help. If there's a grudge currently weighing on you, go to God. Ask Him to help you honestly forgive—and let the healing begin.

Heavenly Father,

The weight of resentment is a heavy weight to carry. I know that, and that is why I come to You, choosing to lay it down before You and ask You to help me forgive. I relinquish my hold on my grudge and instead choose to let it go. With Your help, I will walk in forgiveness.

Amen.

Freedom and Independence

Freedom means I have been set free to become
all that God wants me to be, to achieve all
that God wants me to achieve, to enjoy
all that God wants me to enjoy.

WARREN W. WIERSBE

We have freedom now, because
Christ made us free. So stand strong.

GALATIANS 5:1 NCV

He who trusts in himself is lost.
He who trusts in God can do all things.

SAINT ALPHONSUS LIGUORI

Hold on to God!

Where the Spirit of the Lord is, there is freedom.
2 CORINTHIANS 3:17 NCV

New and exciting changes in life always offer a fresh taste of freedom. The choices and changes that are right around the corner can even seem a little sweeter than in years past, because the direction you choose to go is solely up to you—and God.

Being dependent on God doesn't interfere with that newfound freedom. Relying on God for guidance, strength, comfort, wisdom, and countless other gifts allows you to risk throwing yourself wholeheartedly into the adventure of life. It's like having a partner belay your rope while rock climbing. It gives you the freedom and courage to tackle higher and harder climbs. The closer the "partnership" you have with God, the freer you'll find you are to reach your true potential.

Heavenly Father,

Thank You for the freedom that I have in You and for my newfound freedoms in life. Help me always to remember to rely on You for everything that I need as I leap into the adventure of living out what You call me to do. New and exciting changes await me, but they are even more exciting with You by my side.

Amen.

Fresh Start

The LORD'S love never ends;
his mercies never stop.
They are new every morning.
LAMENTATIONS 3:22–23 NCV

I like sunrises, Mondays, and new seasons.
God seems to be saying, "With me you
can always start afresh."
ADA LUM

If anyone belongs to Christ, there is a new creation.
The old things have gone; everything is made new!
2 CORINTHIANS 5:17 NCV

Brand-New Beginnings

The LORD says,
"I, I am the One who forgives
all your sins, for my sake;
I will not remember your sins."
ISAIAH 43:25 NCV

Many situations in life—graduation, starting a new job, moving out on your own—are brand-new beginnings, a fresh start, a chance to try again or to try something completely new.

These aren't the only fresh starts you'll experience in life, however. God offers you a "beginning-again" ceremony every time you need a second chance. Whenever you blow it, make a poor choice, or even all-out rebel, God says, "Let's begin again." You don't have to go to a job interview or sign a new lease. All God asks is that you come to Him in honest repentance and ask His forgiveness. From that moment, the past truly is history. All is forgiven and your fresh start is ready to commence.

Heavenly Father,

Thank You so much for Your gift of a second chance, a fresh start. No matter how many new beginnings I have in my life, Your forgiveness and grace are more than I could ever need. Help me to come to You every time I need to begin again; I know You will always be there waiting.

Amen.

Friendship

Friendship is the inexpressible comfort of feeling safe with a person, having neither to weigh thoughts nor measure words.

GEORGE ELIOT

A friend loves you all the time.

PROVERBS 17:17 NCV

Friendship is one of the sweetest joys of life. Many might have failed beneath the bitterness of their trial had they not found a friend.

CHARLES HADDON SPURGEON

Friends Old and New

Don't forget your friend.
PROVERBS 27:10 NCV

There are times of change, excitement, expectation ahead—and good-byes. A lot of the people you've grown close to over the past several years may not be headed the same direction that God is leading you. But, that doesn't mean your friendships can't continue to grow.

Keeping in touch across the miles takes effort. However, an e-mail, a crazy card, or a heartfelt phone call is all a friendship needs to spark many happy reunions. The friends that God brings into your life are worth holding on to—and praying for. That includes the ones you haven't met yet. Along with those good-byes, you're also going to be saying a lot of glad-to-meet-yous. So, open your heart. Some of your very best friends are waiting to meet you.

Heavenly Father,

Thank You for the gift of friendships, both old and new. Help me to maintain the godly friendships that You have brought into my life and to be open to all the new friendships that are still waiting to begin. And along the way, help me always to remember that You are the best friend I will ever have.

Amen.

Future

I know the thoughts that I think toward you,
says the LORD, thoughts of peace and not
of evil, to give you a future and a hope.
JEREMIAH 29:11 NKJV

Never be afraid to trust
an unknown future to a known God.
CORRIE TEN BOOM

Wisdom is pleasing to you.
If you find it, you have hope for the future,
and your wishes will come true.
PROVERBS 24:14 NCV

Your Happily Ever After

Good people can look forward to a bright future.
PROVERBS 13:9 NCV

You can only grab hold of the future one day at a time. The rest of it's out of your reach. That doesn't mean you can't look forward to it, plan for it, or even daydream a bit about it. But, the future's like a movie preview of coming attractions. You're only allowed a glimpse of what's to come. The real draw is the main attraction, what's ready for you to experience here and now.

Today is your main attraction, so use it in a way that draws you closer to God. You'll assure yourself of a brighter future—one destined to make a blockbuster of an impact on those around you and ensure you of a happily ever after with the One you love.

Heavenly Father,

The future seems so big and exciting to me! Thank You for everything that's coming up in my life, everything that I have to look forward to. In the meantime, however, help me to maintain my focus on the things You have called me to do today. When I do that, my happily ever after with You will be secure.

Amen.

Generosity

Giving is a joy if we do it in the right spirit.
It all depends on whether we think of it as
"What can I spare?" or as "What can I share?"
ESTHER YORK BURKHOLDER

*Each one should give as you have decided in your heart to give.
You should not be sad when you give, and you should not give
because you feel forced to give. God loves the person who gives happily.
And God can give you more blessings than you need. Then you will
always have plenty of everything—enough to give to every good work.*
2 CORINTHIANS 9:7–8 NCV

You do not have to be rich to be generous.
If he has the spirit of true generosity,
a pauper can give like a prince.
CORRINE U. WELLS

The Path to True Wealth

The generous soul will be made rich,
And he who waters will also be watered himself.

PROVERBS 11:25 NKJV

Picture a miser. Someone like Ebenezer Scrooge will do. He holds on tightly to everything he owns. He's focused on his own needs, the value of his possessions, what he hopes to attain—never on the needs of others. The struggles of those around him do nothing to move his heart. That's because his heart is totally wrapped up in himself.

Now, picture a person whose life is exactly the opposite. That's generosity in action. Holding on to money and possessions loosely. Recognizing that everything one has is a gift, makes it easy to share those gifts with others. That's being other-centered, instead of self-centered.

While being miserly leads to misery, generosity leads to true wealth—the joy of a life rich in relationship, community, and contentment.

Heavenly Father,

Thank You for all of the gifts You have given to me. Your generosity has been endless. I want to be a person who is known for that kind of generosity, not stinginess. Help me to follow in Your footsteps on the path to true wealth, not based on material possessions but in a life lived with You.

Amen.

Gentleness

Walk worthy of the calling with which
you were called, with all lowliness and gentleness,
with longsuffering, bearing with one another in love.

EPHESIANS 4:1–2 NKJV

Power can do by gentleness what
violence fails to accomplish.

LATIN PROVERB

Let everyone see that you are gentle and kind.

PHILIPPIANS 4:5 NCV

Play Gently

Are there those among you who are truly wise and understanding? Then they should show it by living right and doing good things with a gentleness that comes from wisdom.

JAMES 3:13 NCV

Remember wrestling on the floor when you were a kid? The inevitable parental warning usually went something like this: "Don't play rough or someone's going to get hurt!" That same warning holds true today. Anytime you interact with another person, there's a chance that someone may get hurt. That's why being gentle with one another is so important.

It doesn't matter if you're a big, burly guy or a gal who's never met a risk you didn't want to take. Gentleness is not a personality trait. It's a character quality worth putting into practice.

Whomever you spend time with today, friends and strangers alike, play gently. Let your words, your tone of voice, your actions, and even your attitude reflect a tender, godly spirit.

Heavenly Father,

I realize that the people You have placed around me and in my life are human beings made in Your image and worthy of my respect. Help me to always treat other people with gentleness and humility, loving them in the same way that You do.

Amen.

Goals

You become successful the moment you start moving toward a worthwhile goal.
AUTHOR UNKNOWN

I do not mean that I am already as God wants me to be. I have not yet reached that goal, but I continue trying to reach it and to make it mine.
PHILIPPIANS 3:12 NCV

First build a proper goal.
That proper goal will make it easy,
almost automatic, to build a proper you.
JOHANN WOLFGANG VON GOETHE

REALIZING YOUR POTENTIAL

May He grant you according to your heart's desire,
And fulfill all your purpose.
PSALM 20:4 NKJV

Once upon a time, your goal was to graduate, or to get a new job, or to buy a new car. You set your sights on a date, figured out what was required of you, then set mini-goals for completing every individual assignment along the way. Step-by-step you made it to where you wanted to be.

To meet a goal of any kind, you need to have a concrete understanding of what it requires—and of who you are. God can help you do just that. Let Him help you evaluate potential goals that lie ahead and see how they fit with who He created you to be. Then, prioritize the steps it will take to reach your goal in a way that honors Him.

Heavenly Father,

Only in You can I fulfill my true potential. As I begin to set goals for my life and try to attain them, help me to keep my focus on You. When I do that, You will help me discover what would be best for my life and the plan You have for me. I want to set the goals that bring You glory.

Amen.

God's Faithfulness

In God's faithfulness lies eternal security.

CORRIE TEN BOOM

I will sing of the mercies of the LORD forever;
With my mouth will I make known
Your faithfulness to all generations.

PSALM 89:1 NKJV

God is faithful, and if we serve him faithfully,
he will provide for our needs.

SAINT RICHARD OF CHICHESTER

As Good as His Word

*Know that the LORD your God, He is God,
the faithful God who keeps covenant and mercy for a thousand
generations with those who love Him and keep His commandments.*

DEUTERONOMY 7:9 NKJV

Never is a tricky word to use properly. It means no exceptions, no chance, no way—ever. But with God, never is both accurate and encouraging. God never changes. His promises never fail. His patience never falters. His power never diminishes. His love never ends.

All of these things that will never happen with God are the result of His faithfulness. God is as good as His Word. That means you can count on God, even if others have let you down.

Give God the chance to demonstrate His faithfulness to you. Be bold in following through on what you believe He wants you to do. Then, thank Him for the variety of ways He comes through for you.

Heavenly Father,

Thank You so much for Your faithfulness! There is no one in this world who will ever be as faithful to me as You are. Help me to believe in You more and more as I walk through this life, and to trust in Your faithfulness to me in the next.

Amen.

God's Forgiveness

There is only one person God cannot forgive:
the one who refuses to come to him for forgiveness.

AUTHOR UNKNOWN

The LORD is longsuffering and abundant in mercy, forgiving iniquity and transgression.

NUMBERS 14:18 NKJV

God does not wish us to remember what he is willing to forget.

GEORGE ARTHUR BUTTRICK

The Greatest Gift

He has delivered us from the power of darkness and conveyed us into the kingdom of the Son of His love, in whom we have redemption through His blood, the forgiveness of sins.

COLOSSIANS 1:13–14 NKJV

Imagine receiving a gift so overly generous that it leaves you speechless. You've done nothing to earn it. As a matter of fact, at times you've been downright awful to the one who's giving it to you. How does your heart respond?

The forgiveness of God is just such a gift. Your response to that gift, whether you apologize for the past and accept it joyfully with open arms or you bury your head in shame and refuse to take what you don't deserve, is your gift to God. Which will it be?

Right now, kneel before the Giver of all good gifts. Meditate on what He's forgiven in your life and what it cost for Him to offer that free gift to you.

Heavenly Father,

I bow before You, thanking You wholeheartedly for Your forgiveness. I have failed in so many ways, yet You always give me a second chance. Thank You for the gift of Your Son, Jesus, who paid the price for that forgiveness.

Amen.

God's Glory

The glory of God is a living man;
and the life of man consists in beholding God.

SAINT IRENAEUS

The heavens tell the glory of God,
and the skies announce what his hands have made.

PSALM 19:1 NCV

We can almost smell the aroma
of God's beauty in the fresh spring flowers.
His breath surrounds us in the warm summer breezes.

GALE HEIDE

Proclaim It in Your Life!

God once said, "Let the light shine out of the darkness!"
This is the same God who made his light shine in our hearts
by letting us know the glory of God that is in the face of Christ.

2 CORINTHIANS 4:6 NCV

The Bible says that the heavens and the earth proclaim the glory of God. They serve as evidence of His power and majesty. They confirm that He is indeed great enough to handle your life—guiding you to the fulfillment of His plan for you and foiling any foe that might try to obstruct your path.

So look around you and see the glory of your God. Pause and consider the magnificence of a simple flower or the complexity of a common tree. Glance up at the sky and reflect on the fact that God has created an atmosphere capable of sustaining our lives. Look at His handiwork and you will say as He did, "It is good."

Heavenly Father,

Your glory is everywhere I look. From the tiniest of wildflowers to the grandest of mountains, the magnificence of Your creation demonstrates Your power and Your faithfulness. Lord, let Your glory not only be made manifest in the world around me, but also in my life. I want You to shine through me.

Amen.

God's Goodness

The Lord's goodness surrounds us
at every moment. I walk through it almost
with difficulty, as through thick grass and flowers.

R. W. BARBOUR

How great is your goodness
that you have stored up for those who fear you,
that you have given to those who trust you.

PSALM 31:19 NCV

The Infinite Goodness has such wide arms
that it takes whatever turns to it.

DANTE ALIGHIERI

Counting on His Goodness as Your Own

God's goodness will shine down from heaven.
The LORD will give his goodness, and the land will give its crops.
Goodness will go before God and prepare the way for him.

PSALM 85:11–13 NCV

Some people believe that being good will get them into Heaven. But being a "good" man or a "good" woman won't do it. To measure up to God's standard, you must be more than good; you must be perfect—and human beings just aren't capable of that.

That's why God sent His Son, Jesus Christ, to live a life of perfect goodness—a life completely pleasing to God—and then sacrifice that perfect life for you. Don't count on being good enough to spend eternity with God. You'll never make it. Instead, count on the goodness of Christ—God's perfect Son—to get you there.

Heavenly Father,

Thank You so much for the gift of Your perfect Son, Jesus. I know that I am not perfect, but His righteousness becomes mine as I believe in Him and what He did for me on the cross. Fill me with Your goodness, and help me to live a life worthy of His sacrifice for me.

Amen.

God's Love

God soon turns from his wrath,
but he never turns from his love.
CHARLES HADDON SPURGEON

I am persuaded that neither death nor life,
nor angels nor principalities nor powers, nor things present
nor things to come, nor height nor depth, nor any
other created thing, shall be able to separate us
from the love of God which is in Christ Jesus our Lord.
ROMANS 8:38–39 NKJV

Jesus did not come to make God's love possible,
but to make God's love visible.
AUTHOR UNKNOWN

The Most Beautiful "I Love You" Ever

May the Lord lead your hearts
into God's love and Christ's patience.
2 THESSALONIANS 3:5 NCV

"I love you" is a phrase everyone longs to hear. However, real love is evident without a word having to be said. It's seen in the attention, affection, and sacrifice people show for the ones they care about.

If you want to know how much God loves you, just look at what He's done. When Jesus died on the cross, He was saying "I love you" more beautifully than it's ever been said before. But, God's love didn't stop there. He listens to your prayers as if you were the only person in the world. He brings good things into your life, even out of seemingly impossible situations. God's love for you will not end. And your awareness of that love will grow deeper as you grow closer to Him.

Heavenly Father,

Your love is amazing, astounding, and miraculous. You showed Your love for me in Jesus' sacrifice on the cross, and even today, Your love for me continues to be shown through everything You do for me. Thank You so much for loving me all the days of my life.

Amen.

God's Plan for Your Life

God would not have created us
without a specific plan in mind.

ERWIN W. LUTZER

"I know what I am planning for you,"
says the LORD. "I have good plans for you,
not plans to hurt you. I will give you
hope and a good future."

JEREMIAH 29:11 NCV

God's plan, like lilies pure and white, unfold.
We must not tear the close-shut leaves apart.
Time will reveal the calyxes of gold.

MARY RILEY SMITH

Focusing on the Goal

Let us run with endurance the race that is set before us,
looking unto Jesus, the author and finisher of our faith,
who for the joy that was set before Him endured the cross.

HEBREWS 12:1–2 NKJV

Ask any successful runner where he focuses his attention during a race, and he'll tell you he does not watch his competitors, his feet, or the crowd. Rather, his attention stays fixed on the finish line. He focuses on his goal—and that disciplined focus urges him onward till his race is complete.

If you desire to make the most of the life God has given you, you must be able to focus on your goal as well. Ask God to reveal His plan for your life. Ask Him to help you see the markers along the way. Then, lace up your running shoes and go for it. God will be with you throughout the race. And He will be there to present you with your prize when you cross the finish line.

Heavenly Father,

I know that You have only good plans for my life. I ask You to reveal those plans to me, to show me the markers so that I can clearly see, and to help me set the goals that You would have me to reach.

Amen.

God's Power

With God's power working in us,
God can do much, much more than
anything we can ask or imagine.

EPHESIANS 3:20 NCV

Those who walk in God's shadow
are not threatened by the storm.

ANDREA GARNEY

God's power is very great for us who believe.
That power is the same as the great strength God
used to raise Christ from the dead and put him
at his right side in the heavenly world.

EPHESIANS 1:19–20 NCV

God Is in Control of Your Life

He saved them for His name's sake,
That He might make His mighty power known.
PSALM 106:8 NKJV

Some people believe that everything happens for a reason. Others think that life simply happens and God's children are touched with pain and accidents like everyone else. Who's right? That's a question that may not be answered in this life.

What you can be sure of is that God has the power to protect you and He has promised to do so. When you pray, He can do the miraculous to keep you safe. And yet, bad things do happen to good people. It is best to remember that even when you find yourself passing through the valley of the shadow of death, God will be with you. He will walk every inch of that valley with you. And together you will reach the other side.

Heavenly Father,

I know that no matter what happens, You have complete control of my life when I trust in You. Regardless of what the circumstances might seem to declare, nothing can touch me without first going through Your hands. Thank You for Your care over my life.

Amen.

God's Will

I love those who love me,
and those who seek me find me.
Riches and honor are mine to give.
So are wealth and lasting success.
PROVERBS 8:17–18 NCV

Three qualities vital to success:
toil, solitude, prayer.
CARL SANDBURG

Remember the LORD in all you do,
and he will give you success.
PROVERBS 3:6 NCV

God's Will Is Success

Do not be conformed to this world, but be transformed by the renewing of your mind, that you may prove what is that good and acceptable and perfect will of God.

ROMANS 12:2 NKJV

It is God's will for you to succeed both in your spiritual life and in your daily labors. If you excel in your work but neglect your soul, you may end up with every material blessing, but find that none of it satisfies you. If you are deeply spiritual but unsuccessful and struggling in your work, you will be unable to properly provide for your family. God knows that both are important.

Success in one area of your life does not guarantee success in others, so always do your best and pray over every sphere of your life. God wants to bless you in every way. His will is for you to succeed.

Heavenly Father,

I know that real success comes only from You and from following You in every area of my life. I don't want to focus only on material success and fail in other areas such as my physical health, my relationship with others, or my relationship with You. Help me to seek balance and to live that balance out in my life.

Amen.

God's Word

The Bible is God's chart for you to steer by,
to keep you from the bottom of the sea,
and to show you where the harbor is, and how
to reach it without running on rocks and bars.

HENRY WARD BEECHER

Your word is a lamp to my feet
And a light to my path.

PSALM 119:105 NKJV

The Bible is a letter from God
with our personal address on it.

SØREN AABYE KIERKEGAARD

The Highest Standard

All Scripture is given by God and is useful for teaching,
for showing people what is wrong in their lives,
for correcting faults, and for teaching how to live right.
2 TIMOTHY 3:16 NCV

When you come face-to-face with a dilemma—you had a disagreement with a coworker or the media confronts you with a new worldview—you need to know what's right and wrong, what's acceptable and what is not. You need an authoritative standard by which to measure the issues of life.

The Bible is the ultimate Word on what God has determined is truth or error, morally right or wrong. Just as the National Bureau of Standards in Washington, D.C., sets the mark for weights, measurement, time, and mass, so you have a spiritual Bureau of Standards and Measurements—the Bible.

Everything that comes into your life must be placed alongside the Scriptures to see how it measures up.

Heavenly Father,

Thank You that I do not have to wonder about Your will on any matter: You have given me Your Word to help judge situations both in the world and in my own life. Help me to always use the Bible, the Highest Standard, as my measurement in every circumstance.

Amen.

Goodness

God's goodness is the root of all goodness;
and our goodness, if we have any,
springs out of his goodness.
WILLIAM TYNDALE

Examine and see how good the LORD is.
Happy is the person who trusts him.
PSALM 34:8 NCV

Think of how good God is!
He gives us the physical, mental,
and spiritual ability to work in his kingdom,
and then he rewards us for doing it!
ERWIN W. LUTZER

Goodness = Godliness

In the past you offered the parts of your body
to be slaves to sin and evil; ... now you must give
yourselves to be slaves of goodness.
Then you will live only for God.
ROMANS 6:19 NCV

Good seems so relative. Ice cream is good. So are the Broncos. You can have a good attitude, good penmanship, or get a good deal on a used car. Some people even preach, "If it feels good, do it!"

The best way to know what is truly good is to remove an "o" from the word itself. All that remains is God. Whatever God would do, say, or praise in any given situation is what is wholly good.

Being a genuinely good person means being a godly person. That is someone whose heart and actions make God smile. Make that your measure of having a good day.

Heavenly Father,

I want more than to just be a good person; I want to be a godly person—someone who follows Your Word and obeys You in every area of life. I want to be filled with Your goodness so that it flows through me to others, because I know that will make You smile.

Amen.

Grace

Grace is always given to those
ready to give thanks for it.
THOMAS À KEMPIS

*How rich is God's grace, which he has
given to us so fully and freely.*
EPHESIANS 1:7–8 NCV

There is nothing but God's grace.
We walk upon it; we breathe it;
we live and die by it; it makes
the nails and axles of the universe.
ROBERT LOUIS STEVENSON

A Free Gift

If he chose them by grace, it is not for the things they have done.
If they could be made God's people by what they did,
God's gift of grace would not really be a gift.
ROMANS 11:6 NCV

Grace is the ultimate free gift. You don't deserve it. You can't earn it. It will never wear out or grow thin. It fits you perfectly, no matter who you are. All you have to do to receive this life-changing gift is ask for it.

The gift of grace is free, but that doesn't mean it didn't come at a high price. God asked Jesus to give His life so that grace could change not only your destiny here on Earth but also for eternity. He believed you were worth it.

Take a moment to think about God's gift of grace—and what it cost to extend it so freely to you. Thank God for the difference it's made in your life.

Heavenly Father,

Thank You so much for believing in me, long before I ever knew You existed. You sent Your Son to die on the cross for me—the greatest gift of grace I will ever receive. Help me to never forget all that You have done for me.

Amen.

Growth

Progress in the Christian life is exactly equal to the growing knowledge we gain of the Triune God in personal experience.

A. W. TOZER

Good people will grow like palm trees. ...
Like trees planted in the Temple of the LORD,
they will grow strong in the courtyards of our God.
When they are old, they will still produce fruit.

PSALM 92:12–14 NCV

Gradual growth in grace, knowledge, faith, love, holiness, humility, and spiritual-mindedness—*all this I see clearly taught and urged in Scripture.*

J. C. RYLE

Rooted in the Truth

As you therefore have received Christ Jesus the Lord, so walk in Him, rooted and built up in Him and established in the faith.
COLOSSIANS 2:6–7 NKJV

As you grow older, your place in the world changes. You're finally considered a grown-up, or at least regarded as approaching that designation. But, being "grown" doesn't mean you stop growing. Every single day of your life, from the moment you were conceived until the day you meet Jesus face-to-face, you're growing into who God created you to be.

Just like any thriving plant—or person—how well you grow is partially dependent on the quality of the soil you're planted in. When you're firmly rooted in what God has to say about you, you can withstand any type of weather. So, when the storms start to blow, dig down deep into what you know is true.

Heavenly Father,

As I grow older, the more my life changes. Exciting opportunities await me as I become a "grown up," and I can hardly wait for my life as a real adult to begin. Even in the midst of these changes, help me to keep my focus on You so that even as I "grow up" outwardly, I am also growing up inwardly, with my roots based in Your Word.

Amen.

Guidance

The teacher of teachers gives his guidance noiselessly.
I have never heard him speak, and yet I know
that he is within me. At every moment he
instructs me and guides me. And whenever
I am in need of it, he enlightens me afresh.

THERESE OF LISIEUX

I am continually with You;
You hold me by my right hand.
You will guide me with Your counsel.

PSALM 73:23–24 NKJV

I know not the way God leads me,
but well do I know my Guide.

MARTIN LUTHER

GPS for Life

The LORD says, "I will make you wise and show you where to go. I will guide you and watch over you."

PSALM 32:8 NCV

A Global Positioning System for your life would make a great gift. You could type in your goals—where you want to go—and a friendly voice would advise you as to the best way to get there.

Your relationship with God is better than any GPS on the market. God knows where you've been, where you are, and which direction is best for you to head in the future. God wants you to have access to that same useful information. By reading the Bible, weighing advice from godly friends, and asking God's Spirit to guide you in prayer, you have access to a system of guidance that will never fail, no matter where you roam.

Heavenly Father,

You are better than any GPS man could ever create. You know better than anyone else the best path for my life. Help me to hear Your voice clearly so that You can point me in the right direction. As I follow Your will for my life, I know You will guide me where I need to go.

Amen.

Healing

Man is rather an upstanding human being whose vision has been impaired by the cataracts of sin and whose soul has been weakened by the virus of pride, but there is sufficient vision left for him to lift his eyes unto the hills, and there remains enough of God's image for him to turn his weak and sin-battered life toward the Great Physician, the curer of the ravages of sin.

MARTIN LUTHER

Christ carried our sins in his body on the cross so we would stop living for sin and start living for what is right. And you are healed because of his wounds.

1 PETER 2:24 NCV

No one ever looks in vain to the Great Physician.

F. F. BOSWORTH

Seeking Out the Great Physician

Jesus said, "It is not the healthy people who need a doctor,
but the sick. I have not come to invite good people
but sinners to change their hearts and lives."

LUKE 5:31 NCV

When Jesus and His disciples walked through the hill country of Nazareth, He ministered to all who came to Him. He touched those who needed healing and made them well. He healed those whose minds were sick and failing. But Jesus also spoke of those who needed spiritual healing—those whose souls were sick with sin and on the verge of spiritual death. Jesus brought healing to every part of His followers' lives.

Perhaps your body is fit and healthy, your mind quick and strong, but you have no relationship with God. Your spirit has been mortally wounded and only God can make you whole again. Seek Him out. Tell Him what you need. He's the Great Physician.

Heavenly Father,

I thank You that You are my Great Physician. You know my body better than any doctor ever could, because You created me. I know that Your will is that I walk in health—both physically and spiritually. Thank You for Your healing power that cures any disease that I have.

Amen.

Health

Our Substitute bore both our sins and our sicknesses that we might be delivered from them.

F. F. BOSWORTH

I am the LORD who heals you.

EXODUS 15:26 NKJV

It has been scientifically proven that worry, discord, and melancholy undermine health. Good spirits make for good digestion. Cheerfulness costs nothing; yet is beyond price.

B. C. FORBES

The Lord Who Heals You

You shall serve the LORD your God, and
He will bless your bread and your water.
And I will take sickness away from the midst of you.
EXODUS 23:25 NKJV

Your body is an incredible gift, but it's not an indestructible one. Bodies break down, wear out, and catch all kinds of diseases. Even if you take good care of yourself—eat a balanced diet, get enough sleep, exercise regularly—your body may not always run smoothly.

When your health goes downhill, get God involved. He doesn't discourage you from seeking medical treatment. He simply encourages you to turn to Him as part of the healing process. God wants you to be healthy and whole in every area of your life—body, soul and spirit. Trust Him to help you reach healing in the way He knows is best.

Heavenly Father,

I thank You so much that You are the great Lord who heals me from every disease and ailment I could ever encounter. I commit to aiding You in this process by taking good care of my body. And I know that the things that I cannot control, You will help because You desire that my body be well in every area.

Amen.

Heaven

Heaven is a prepared place
for a prepared people.
LEWIS SPERRY CHAFER

*We know that our body—the tent we live
in here on earth—will be destroyed.
But when that happens, God will have a house for us.
It will not be a house made by human hands;
instead, it will be a home in heaven that will last forever.*
2 CORINTHIANS 5:1 NCV

Heaven will be the perfection we have
always longed for. All the things that made
earth unlovely and tragic will be absent in heaven.
BILLY GRAHAM

Welcome Home!

Jesus said, "There are many rooms
in my Father's house. ... I am going there
to prepare a place for you."
JOHN 14:2 NCV

All of us who have experienced a graduation know that it is a combination of ceremony, excitement, endings, and brand-new beginnings. It's usually a celebration that's hard to forget. But, there's another graduation day ahead, one you may be a little more hesitant to participate in. That's the day you graduate to life after death.

It's a little unnerving not knowing what to expect. But, one thing is certain. God's been waiting for that day with greater expectation than you had about saying good-bye to your toughest class. He's prepared a place just for you, a place where you truly belong.

Anytime the fear of death grabs hold of your heart, just picture meeting God face-to-face and hearing Him say with a smile, "Welcome home!"

Heavenly Father,

I must admit that at times I am a little hesitant to "graduate" to the life You have for me after death. But I know that because You are busy preparing a special place for me in my heavenly home, I have no reason to fear. Thank You for always being with me. I look forward to coming home and being with You.

Amen.

Help

Lord, help me to remember that nothing is going
to happen to me today that you and I cannot handle.

AUTHOR UNKNOWN

The LORD has heard my cry for help;
the LORD will answer my prayer.

PSALM 6:9 NCV

When faced with a mountain, I will not quit!
I will keep on striving until I climb over,
find a pass through, tunnel underneath ...
or simply stay and turn the mountain
into a gold mine, with God's help.

ROBERT HAROLD SCHULLER

S.O.S!

We can be sure when we say,
"I will not be afraid, because the Lord is my helper.
People can't do anything to me."
HEBREWS 13:6 NCV

Help! A simple one-word prayer is often the most heartfelt. But, brevity doesn't bother God. He knows exactly what's behind your desperate plea. He also knows exactly what you need—and it may differ considerably from what you want. You may want circumstances to change immediately, even time to reverse itself.

Though God can, and does, work miracles, usually His help comes in subtler ways—through a renewal of strength, an outpouring of hope, or a peace that passes understanding. It may come through the words of a friend, the kindness of a stranger, or the awesome wonder of a thunderstorm. The help God offers varies from situation to situation. But, one thing that never varies is God's dependability in answering your heartfelt prayer.

Heavenly Father,

There are times when my most honest prayer is a simple one: Help! Sometimes life can be overwhelming and I have nowhere else to turn. That's when I send out an S.O.S. to You. Thank You for always standing ready to help with whatever I need. You are a great and present help in times of trouble.

Amen.

Honesty

I consider the most enviable of all titles,
the character of an honest man.

GEORGE WASHINGTON

Light shines on those who do right;
joy belongs to those who are honest.

PSALM 97:11 NCV

Honesty has a beautiful and refreshing simplicity about it. No ulterior motives. No hidden meanings.

CHARLES R. SWINDOLL

Breaking the Habit of Dishonesty

The LORD does what is right, and he loves justice,
so honest people will see his face.
PSALM 11:7 NCV

You don't have to be on the FBI's Most Wanted List to be dishonest. All you have to do is exaggerate a personal story to make yourself look better in your friends' eyes. Eat a few grapes before you pay for the bunch at the grocery store. Or record your weight a few pounds lower than reality on a health insurance form.

Dishonesty is a habit that's easy to develop. Honesty is not so easy, but it is a gift to the God who loves you. It tells Him that He can trust you. And it tells you that you can trust yourself. Honesty may stir up some waves on the surface of your life, but deep down in the depths of your soul, it produces genuine, lasting peace.

Heavenly Father,

I want to live a life that is characterized by truth and integrity. I know I can't do it on my own. Please help me to be honest in every area of my life, to set the standard of integrity high so that I can live a life that is pleasing to You.

Amen.

Hope

Do not look to your hope,
but to Christ, the source of your hope.
CHARLES HADDON SPURGEON

Be of good courage,
And He shall strengthen your heart,
All you who hope in the LORD.
PSALM 31:24 NKJV

There is no medicine like hope,
no incentive so great, and no tonic
so powerful as expectation
of something tomorrow.
SAMUEL JOHNSON

Holding Fast to Hope

I pray that the God who gives hope will fill you
with much joy and peace while you trust in him.
Then your hope will overflow by the power of the Holy Spirit.
HEBREWS 15:13 NCV

Hope is the perfect life preserver in the midst of any storm. It helps keep your head above water, enabling you to fight off feelings of discouragement and despair. As you catch an occasional glimpse of what lies beyond the waves, it aids in reminding you that help is on the way, even if you can't quite see it yet. Hope helps you survive.

When storm clouds are gathering on the horizon, or if a torrential downpour has caught you by surprise, hold fast to hope. Remember how God came through time and time again for people in the Bible. Think about how He's come through for you. Then, meditate on His steadfast promises, your greatest source of hope. Help is on its way.

Heavenly Father,

Sometimes life can be so overwhelming and there is darkness on all sides. This is when I need to remember all the times You have been there for me before and how You have always brought me through. Help me to hold on to the hope that I have in You.

Amen.

Hospitality

Who practices hospitality
entertains God himself.
AUTHOR UNKNOWN

*Open your homes to each other,
without complaining.*
1 PETER 4:9 NCV

When there is room in the heart,
there is room in the house.
DANISH PROVERB

A Welcoming Attitude

Be kindly affectionate to one another ... given to hospitality.
ROMANS 12:10, 13 NKJV

You don't have to own a house to make someone feel at home. All you have to do is open your heart. That's what hospitality is all about. It has nothing to do with your gourmet cooking skills or opulent guest accommodations. Cheerfully sharing what you have—be it little or much—is the only rule.

So, relax. Welcome in friends both old and new. Ask lots of questions and listen thoughtfully to their answers. Don't try to impress visitors with your immaculate housekeeping or culinary expertise. Warm them with genuine care and affection. The more you see guests—even unexpected ones—as a blessing instead of an inconvenience, the more you'll enjoy the adventure of opening your home, and heart, to others.

Heavenly Father,

I want to be the kind of person who has a welcoming heart toward other people. Whether I have little or much, help me to be willing to share it with those whom You bring across my path. I want all who enter my home to experience Your peace, love, and joy as we fellowship and break bread together. Thank You for Your example of hospitality and for welcoming me into Your family.

Amen.

Humility

It is no great thing to be humble when you
are brought low; but to be humble when you
are praised is a great and rare attainment.
SAINT BERNARD OF CLAIRVAUX

*Do not think you are better than you are. ...
In Christ we are all one body. Each one
is a part of that body, and each part belongs
to all the other parts. We all have different gifts,
each of which came because of the grace God gave us.*
ROMANS 12:3, 5–6 NCV

If you are humble, nothing
will touch you, neither praise nor disgrace,
because you know what you are.
MOTHER TERESA

Getting a Clear View of Yourself

Be clothed with humility, for
"God resists the proud,
But gives grace to the humble."
1 PETER 5:5 NKJV

Unlike what you see in the movies, humility is a good thing. It isn't putting yourself down or trying to blend in with the wallpaper. Humility is simply seeing yourself from God's point of view. It's accepting that you're worth no more, or less, than any other person whom God dearly loves.

Once you have a clear view of yourself, you can get a clearer view of what God wants you to do. You won't argue over what you think is too hard for you to tackle or way beneath your dignity. You can do whatever God asks—and rest in knowing that with God, your best is always good enough.

Heavenly Father,

Thank You for the gift of humility. Help me to always see myself from Your perspective—no better, or worse, than I really am. I know I am not perfect; I am a work in progress. As I keep that in mind, I know that You are working in my life to make me who You want me to be.

Amen.

Identity

The Spirit we received does not make us slaves again to fear; it makes us children of God. With that Spirit we cry out, "Father." And the Spirit himself joins with our spirits to say we are God's children.

ROMANS 8:15–16 NCV

He who counts the stars and calls them by their names is in no danger of forgetting His own children.

CHARLES HADDON SPURGEON

If anyone is in Christ, he is a new creation; old things have passed away; behold, all things have become new.

2 CORINTHIANS 5:17 NKJV

Getting to Know the Real You

It is no longer I who live, but Christ lives in me; and the life which I now live in the flesh I live by faith in the Son of God, who loved me and gave Himself for me.

GALATIANS 2:20 NKJV

Way back in the 1960s, young adults were obsessed with "finding themselves." To accomplish this, they experimented with things like drugs, communal living, and transcendental meditation. Unfortunately, these are ways to lose yourself.

What was true in the sixties is true today. There's only one way to find your true identity—believe what God has to say about you. God says you're loved, forgiven, unique, and eternally significant. As His child, you're also part of a new family that is destined to make a positive impact on this world and the next.

Take a moment to thank God for the many ways He's helping you "find yourself" in Him.

Heavenly Father,

I don't want to lose myself in the search to find myself. Thank You that You want to help me get to know the real me—the one who is loved and forgiven, created as one of a kind with unique gifts and a purpose that only I can fulfill. Thank You that I can find my identity in You.

Amen.

Influence

Immortality lies not in the things
you leave behind, but in the people
your life has touched.
AUTHOR UNKNOWN

*Be an example to the believers
with your words, your actions,
your love, your faith, and your pure life.*
1 TIMOTHY 4:12 NCV

We can influence others as much
as God has influenced us.
BOBBIE-JEAN MERCK

Making a Difference

Do everything without complaining or arguing.
Then you will be innocent and without any wrong.
You will be God's children without fault. But you are
living with crooked and mean people all around you,
among whom you shine like stars in the dark world.

PHILIPPIANS 2:14–15 NCV

You are a walking, talking message of hope. Whether you realize it or not, your character, words, and actions are all preaching a sermon to those you meet along the road of life. The closer you follow God, the more visible He'll be to others through you.

You may never know how wide your influence really goes. An act of kindness, a word of encouragement, or a job well done could be what moves a close friend, or even a stranger, one step closer to knowing God.

Take a moment to thank God for the people who've had a positive influence on your life. Then, ask God to help you become someone else's reason for thanks.

Heavenly Father,

It's sometimes hard to tell when I am making a difference in another person's life. In the midst of daily life it's easy to forget that I am a walking, talking billboard for You. Help me to be a good influence in the lives of those whom You place in my path.

Amen.

Integrity

Integrity is not a conditional word.
It doesn't blow in the wind or change
with the weather. It is your inner image
of yourself, and if you look in there
and see a man who won't cheat,
then you know he never will.

JOHN D. MACDONALD

You uphold me in my integrity,
And set me before Your face forever.

PSALM 41:12 NKJV

There is no such thing as
a minor lapse of integrity.

TOM PETERS

Standing Up to the Pressure

Let integrity and uprightness preserve me,
For I wait for You.
PSALM 25:21 NKJV

When storms begin to blow, the integrity of a building is revealed—the strength of its foundation, the practicality of its design, and the quality of its building materials. Will it stand or will it fall?

The same holds true for your own integrity. When the pressure is on, weak spots in your faith or character readily come to light. If this happens, take note. Your integrity matures over time. If you've made choices that weren't sound in the past, make better choices today. Make sure your foundation rests solely on what God says is true, not on what your emotions or contemporary culture says is right and fair.

Then, turn your face toward the wind with confidence. You, and your integrity, are built to last.

Heavenly Father,

It is not in the easy times but in times of hardship and pressure that I see what I am made of. Help me to be a person of integrity not only when things are going smoothly, but when the difficulties of life arise. Thank You for Your help to stand strong.

Amen.

Joy

Joy is the most infallible sign
of the presence of God.
LEON BLOY

Jesus said, "Ask and you will receive,
so that your joy will be the fullest joy."
JOHN 16:24 NCV

Life need not be easy to be joyful.
Joy is not the absence of trouble
but the presence of Christ.
WILLIAM VAN DER HOVEN

Getting to Know the Source of Joy

LORD, you have made me happy by what you have done;
I will sing for joy about what your hands have done.
PSALM 92:4 NCV

When a baby sees his mother's face, every part of his body wiggles, jiggles, and smiles with delight. His source of joy is the one he loves, the one he recognizes—even at an early age—the one who loves him in return.

Growing in your relationship with God is not just an exercise in getting to know the Bible better. It is all about getting to know God better, up close and personal. He wants to be the source of your joy and delight.

Even when circumstances are anything but happy, true joy is as close as God's loving presence. Spend time talking to Him, finding comfort in His promises and contentment in His love. There is no deeper joy this side of heaven.

Heavenly Father,

Thank You that my joy is not based on outward circumstances, but on my relationship with You, which will never change. No matter what happens in my life, I know that I can count on You to bring me true and lasting joy.

Amen.

Justice

Defend the poor and fatherless;
Do justice to the afflicted and needy.

PSALM 82:3 NKJV

To sin by silence when they should protest makes cowards of men.

ABRAHAM LINCOLN

We will not be satisfied until justice rolls down like waters, and righteousness like a mighty stream.

MARTIN LUTHER KING, JR.

Standing Up for What's Right

The King is powerful and loves justice.
LORD, you made things fair;
you have done what is fair and right
PSALM 99:4 NCV

When you see a friend being harassed or taken advantage of and you speak up about it, you're striving for what's right and just. When a con artist defrauds an elderly lady of her life savings and you call the authorities, it's justice you're seeking.

God is a God of justice. He doesn't turn a blind eye to injustice, and He doesn't want you to. Speaking up or doing something when you see wrong being done is a God-given instinct. Just be sure that it's justice that you seek and not "an-eye-for-an-eye" revenge.

Once you've done what you can, leave matters in the hands of those in authority. And most importantly, always leave them in the hands of God.

Heavenly Father,

Thank You that You are a God of justice and I can always count on You to do what's right. As I live my life following You and Your ways, help me to remember that ultimately You are the One who is in charge, and You will always set things straight.

Amen.

Kindness

Be the living expression of God's kindness:
kindness in your face, kindness in your eyes,
kindness in your smile, kindness in your warm greeting.

MOTHER TERESA

Worry is a heavy load, but
a kind word cheers you up.

PROVERBS 12:25 NCV

Constant kindness can accomplish much.
As the sun makes ice melt, kindness
causes misunderstanding,
mistrust and hostility to evaporate.

ALBERT SCHWEITZER

Give the Gift of Kindness

To your service for God, add kindness
for your brothers and sisters in Christ;
and to this kindness, add love.

2 PETER 1:7 NCV

Kindness is not always soft, quiet, and cuddly. Sometimes it boldly speaks the words someone needs to hear. It stands up for what's right, even when what's right isn't what's popular. Kindness does whatever it takes to do what's in the best interest of another.

What gives kindness its gentle strength is love. Every word and action, whether meeting the physical needs of a stranger or confronting a friend on her tendency toward unhealthy behaviors, is motivated by other-centered compassion. Kindness is sensitive to different personality types, creatively crafting an appropriate response for each unique situation. It always leaves pride and judgment behind and reaches out with open, accepting arms to tenderly help another move closer to God. How can you put kindness into action today?

Heavenly Father,

Kindness so often gets a bad rap in this day and age. But kindness is a choice, an indication of strength of character that is willing to put the needs of others first. Help me to walk in kindness toward other people, not just my friends and family, but everyone who comes across my path.

Amen.

Knowledge

Grow in the grace and knowledge
of our Lord and Savior Jesus Christ.

2 PETER 3:18 NCV

Knowledge is indispensable to Christian life and service. If we do not use the mind that God has given us, we condemn ourselves to spiritual superficiality and cut ourselves off from many of the riches of God's grace. Knowledge is given us to be used, to lead us to higher worship, greater faith, deeper holiness, better service.

JOHN STOTT

Do what God's teaching says;
when you only listen and do nothing,
you are fooling yourselves.

JAMES 1:23 NCV

Use It or Lose It

Incline your ear and hear the words of the wise,
And apply your heart to my knowledge;
PROVERBS 22:17 NKJV

How much do you know? Do you have a diploma on your wall or some hard-learned life lessons to your credit? If so, make sure that learning continues to work for you.

Putting what you know into practice will help you retain the information you have worked so hard to acquire. If you put what you've learned on the shelf, chances are it will be more or less forgotten as time goes by.

The "use it or lose it" principle is true of your knowledge of God as well. If you put God and the Bible on the shelf for a while, you may have to relearn some hard lessons. Who wants to take calculus, or a painful lesson on pride, over again? Put what you know into practice.

Heavenly Father,

As my life continues to change as I seek success along my chosen path, help me to always remember that knowledge from the world is not enough. I want to increase my knowledge of You, and put it into practice in my life.

Amen.

Life

Jesus said, "I am the way, and the truth, and the life. The only way to the Father is through me."

JOHN 14:6 NCV

However far you go, it is not much use if it is not in the right direction.

WILLIAM BARCLAY

Give yourselves completely to God. Stand against the devil, and the devil will run from you. Come near to God, and God will come near to you.

JAMES 4:7–8 NCV

The Journey of Life

I am offering you life or death, blessings or curses. Now, choose life! Then you and your children may live. To choose life is to love the LORD your God, obey him, and stay close to him. He is your life.

DEUTERONOMY 30:19–20 NCV

What is the meaning of life? This question has been debated by philosophy classes for centuries. But, guess what? You know the answer. Life is a journey toward, or away from, the heart of God. Keeping that in mind makes even the most ordinary day seem extraordinarily important. And it is.

What you do with today matters. Whether you're riding roller coasters with friends or feeding the hungry at a soup kitchen doesn't matter as much as whether what you're doing is drawing you closer to, or farther away from, the One who loves you most.

Where will life take you today? The direction is up to you.

Heavenly Father,

I realize that my life only counts as I live it for You. Each day that I live on this planet is important in Your plan for me. Help me to remember every day to make choices that will honor You and bring me closer to You.

Amen.

Love

Dear friends, we should love each other,
because love comes from God. Everyone who loves
has become God's child and knows God.
Whoever does not love does not know
God, because God is love.

1 JOHN 4:7–8 NCV

He who is filled with love
is filled with God himself.

SAINT AUGUSTINE OF HIPPO

Love is patient and kind. Love is not jealous,
it does not brag, and it is not proud. Love is not rude,
is not selfish, and does not get upset with others.
Love does not count up wrongs that have been done.

1 CORINTHIANS 13:4–5 NCV

What Love Looks Like

No one has ever seen God, but if we love each other,
God lives in us, and his love is made perfect in us.
1 JOHN 4:12 NCV

Want to know what love looks like? Look at God. Consider His sacrifice, His patience, His comfort, His faithfulness, His generosity. God's creativity in expressing love is so great that it's almost incomprehensible.

Consider how your love stands up next to His. Don't get discouraged. You're not God. At times, your love still falters and fails. But, God's love is at work in your life. He's helping you love others in the same wonderful way He so deeply loves you.

Let God's creative compassion inspire you to love others well. Ask for His help in knowing the best way to express your love so that it meets needs, builds relationships, and warms hearts. Then, take a moment to sit back and enjoy His love for you.

Heavenly Father,

Thank You for Your amazing love that teaches me how to love other people. I want to love others the way that You love them. Help me find ways to reach out to them and express my love in the way that people need it the most.

Amen.

Meditation

In the rush and noise of life,
as you have intervals, step home
within yourselves and be still.
Wait upon God, and feel his
good presence; this will
carry you evenly through
your day's business.

WILLIAM PENN

Meditate within your heart
on your bed, and be still.

PSALM 4:4 NKJV

Meditation is the activity of calling
to mind, and thinking over, and dwelling on,
and applying to oneself, the various things
that one knows about the works and ways
and purposes and promises of God.

J. I. PACKER

Meditating on God

I will meditate on the glorious splendor
of Your majesty, And on Your wondrous works.
PSALM 145:5 NKJV

Meditation gets a bad rap. It gets tied in with the New Age movement, Eastern religion, even weight-loss programs. But, way back in Old Testament times, God told people to meditate. The key was what He told them to meditate on—Him.

Meditating on God—His character, His miracles, and His words as communicated in the Bible—helps you understand more about what God is really like. It helps change your thinking and even your behavior, from the inside out.

Set aside five uninterrupted minutes today to mediate on God. Choose one quality of God's character and think about the difference it makes in your life. Let it lead you to thanks, to praise, and closer to the heart of God Himself.

Heavenly Father,

Your Word tells me of all the wonderful things You have done and what an amazing God You are. I want to spend my time thinking and meditating on Your Word as well as all of the miraculous things You have done in my own life. Thank You for everything You do for me.

Amen.

Mercy

Nothing graces the Christian
soul as much as mercy.
SAINT AMBROSE

*You must show mercy to others,
or God will not show mercy
to you when he judges you.
But the person who shows mercy
can stand without fear
at the judgment.*
JAMES 2:13 NCV

Two works of mercy set a man free:
forgive and you will be forgiven,
and give and you will receive.
SAINT AUGUSTINE OF HIPPO

The Gift That Sets Us Free

What does the LORD require of you
But to do justly, To love mercy,
And to walk humbly with your God?
MICAH 6:8 NKJV

Mercy is the key that sets a prisoner free. It extends grace in place of judgment, forgiveness in place of punishment, and honor in place of disdain. It makes no sense, except to a heart filled with God's unconditional love.

Mercy is a gift God asks you to give to others—not because they deserve it, but because of the mercy God has demonstrated in your own life. Ask God to bring to mind anyone who could use a tender touch of mercy. Depending on how God leads you to bestow this special gift, the one who receives it may never even be fully aware of its extent. But, you will. You'll find that being merciful frees up your own heart to love more authentically.

Heavenly Father,

Thank You for the gift of Your mercy that sets me free. I want to be a person who bestows mercy and unconditional love on other people. Help me not to make quick judgments but to practice mercy in every area of my life.

Amen.

Nature

I love to think of nature as an unlimited
broadcasting station through which
God speaks to us every hour, if we will only tune in.

GEORGE WASHINGTON CARVER

Every beast of the forest is Mine,
And the cattle on a thousand hills.
I know all the birds of the mountains,
And the wild beasts of the field are Mine.

PSALM 50:10–11 NKJV

The more I study nature, the more
I am amazed at the Creator.

LOUIS PASTEUR

The Work of an Artist

God looked at everything he
had made, and it was very good.
GENESIS 1:31 NCV

To better understand the heart of an artist, you need to study his work. Examine his brush strokes. Note his favorite color palette. Consider his subject matter. Just sit and enjoy the beauty of his creation.

God is the ultimate Artist. His creations are so amazing that a lifetime is not long enough to fully appreciate them. However, you can understand God's heart a little better by studying His work. Even the simplest flower shows His creativity, attention to detail, organizational skills, and love of beauty.

Wherever you are right now, take a quick peek outside. What does what you see teach you about the God you cannot see? Take a moment to tell God what you think about His handiwork.

Heavenly Father,

You are the Master Artist, and nature is Your masterpiece. I stand in awe before Your creation, amazed at the work of Your hands. As I go throughout my daily life, help me not to forget that Your love for me is demonstrated all around. I just need to open my eyes and look.

Amen.

Patience

Teach us, O Lord, the disciplines of patience,
for to wait is often harder than to work.

PETER MARSHALL

Patient people have great understanding, but people with quick tempers show their foolishness.

PROVERBS 14:29 NCV

Be patient with everyone,
but above all, with yourself.

SAINT FRANCIS DE SALES

Learning to Wait

Rest in the LORD, and wait patiently for Him.
PSALM 37:7 NKJV

Waiting at a red light can drive you nuts. It seems like wasted time—especially if you happen to be in a hurry. But, life is filled with metaphorical red lights. Some of them God puts right in front of you on purpose—to slow you down, so you'll wait on Him.

Waiting for God's "green light" in any situation teaches you patience. It reminds you that some things are simply out of your control. It prompts you to stay close in prayer. It protects you by giving you time to mature. It opens your eyes to things you might have missed in your hurry to move further and faster down the road of life. As you're waiting patiently, God is working purposefully.

Heavenly Father,

Life is full of red lights, and they can be so aggravating and frustrating! I need more of Your patience in every situation that I face. Help me to slow down and wait and enjoy the things around me as I do. I know that You will work wonders in my life as I wait patiently for You.

Amen.

Peace

No God, no peace.
Know God, know peace.
AUTHOR UNKNOWN

You, LORD, give true peace to those
who depend on you, because they trust you.
ISAIAH 26:3 NCV

Christ alone can bring lasting peace—
peace with God—peace among men
and nations—and peace within our hearts.
BILLY GRAHAM

Peace in Any Situation

Jesus said, "Peace I leave with you, My peace I give to you; not as the world gives do I give to you. Let not your heart be troubled, neither let it be afraid."

JOHN 14:27 NKJV

As every beauty-pageant contestant seems to agree, peace—world peace—is one of the deepest desires of the human heart. But what's less frequently understood is that peace is not determined by location or situation. Peace will blanket the world only when Jesus Christ is Lord of all nations and every heart is surrendered to Him.

War, relational conflict, and inner turmoil are all part of life on this earth. But, that doesn't mean you can't have perfect peace in your own heart. It's available right now. Ask God to give you a taste of what true peace is like, as you trust in His goodness and rest in His presence.

Heavenly Father,

Peace seems so hard to come by in a world filled with turmoil and conflict. But I know that Your true peace can come no matter what situation I find myself in. In every circumstance, help me to experience the peace that passes all understanding.

Amen.

Perseverance

Permanence, perseverance, and persistence
in spite of all obstacles, discouragements,
and impossibilities—it is this that in all things
distinguishes the strong soul from the weak.

SIR FRANCIS DRAKE

We must not become tired of doing good.
We will receive our harvest of eternal life
at the right time if we do not give up.

GALATIANS 6:9 NCV

There must be a beginning to any great matter,
but the continuing to the end until it be
thoroughly finished yields the true glory.

THOMAS CARLYLE

Never Give Up

Let us run the race before us and never give up.

HEBREWS 12:1 NCV

In track and field, there are a few commonsense tips to winning a race: Stay in shape. Stay alert. Pace yourself. Keep your eyes on the goal. Never give up.

Life can feel like a very long race at times. It's easy to get tired or discouraged when obstacles get in your way or when it feels as though the people running next to you would rather see you fail than succeed. But, God has a race that's set just for you. It's not a saunter through the park. It's a race that will push you to your full potential. Keep moving. God's cheering you on every step of the way.

Heavenly Father,

I want to be known as a person who has perseverance, someone who never gives up. Though my life often feels like a marathon and it is hard to keep going at times, I commit to pressing on and reaching my full potential in You. Thank You for Your help in reaching all of my goals.

Amen.

Praise

Let everything that
has breath praise the LORD.
Praise the LORD!

PSALM 150:6 NKJV

Receive every day as a resurrection
from death, as a new enjoyment of life . . .
let your joyful heart praise and magnify
so good and glorious a Creator.

WILLIAM LAW

He put a new song in my mouth,
a song of praise to our God.
Many people will see this and worship him.
Then they will trust the LORD.

PSALM 40:3 NCV

Worthy of Our Praise

[The LORD] is the one you should praise; he is your God, who has done great and wonderful things for you, which you have seen with your own eyes.

DEUTERONOMY 10:21 NCV

What a wonderful God we serve! He is always loving, always faithful, always patient, always forgiving, and always true. Our God is all-knowing, all-powerful, and ever present. There is nothing He cannot do, no prayer He cannot answer, no void He cannot fill.

God is worthy of your praise—innately, overwhelmingly worthy. Open your heart and give Him His due. As you do, you'll find your life changed, your problems conquered, your joy overflowing. Nothing can compare to the epiphany of knowing that your God is able to keep all His promises to you.

So praise Him and keep praising Him. Worship Him and keep worshipping Him. Love Him and keep loving Him. The more you pour out on Him, the more you will receive from Him in return. He will never let you down.

Heavenly Father,

You are worthy of my praise! I am so thankful for everything You have done for me and for who You are in my life. Thank You for keeping Your promises, for being so faithful, for loving me for who I am. I will praise You for the rest of my life.

Amen.

Prayer

We should speak to God
from our own hearts
and talk to him as a child
talks to his father.

CHARLES HADDON SPURGEON

Pray without ceasing.

1 THESSALONIANS 5:17 NKJV

When you can't put your prayers
into words, God hears your heart.

AUTHOR UNKNOWN

Anytime Is the Right Time

The LORD says, "It shall come to pass
That before they call, I will answer; And while
they are still speaking, I will hear."
ISAIAH 65:24 NKJV

You don't need words to talk to God. Tears, sighs, and even silence can communicate with your Heavenly Father in the same way that a look on your face can communicate what you're feeling to a friend. Those who know you well can understand what runs even deeper than words, just by being in your presence.

The Creator of the universe is always in your presence—although that's easy to forget at times. Even though He knows your every thought, prayer reminds you that God is near. It prompts you to include Him in every aspect of your day, even in the little details.

When you wake up, before you fall asleep, whether you're feeling fearful or joyful ... anytime is the right time to talk to God.

Heavenly Father,

Sometimes I get so busy in my daily life that I forget to communicate with You. Thank You that You are always with me, no matter where I am or what I am doing. Help me to include You in every aspect of my life. I know that anytime is the right time to breathe a prayer to You.

Amen.

Priorities

When you put God first,
you are establishing order
for everything else in your life.
ANDREA GARNEY

Jesus said, "Seek first the kingdom of God and His righteousness, and all these things shall be added to you."
MATTHEW 6:33 NKJV

Tell me to what you pay attention,
and I will tell you who you are.
JOSÉ ORTEGA Y GASSET

Making God Number One

Jesus said, "No one can serve two masters. The person will hate one master and love the other, or will follow one master and refuse to follow the other. You cannot serve both God and worldly riches."

MATTHEW 6:24 NCV

How you live your life reflects your true priorities more than any list you may be holding in your head. Suppose your love for others is evident to those who know you—and even those who don't. Suppose you talk to God about both the small things as well as the big ones you face each and every day. And suppose you make plans for your future based on the big picture of eternity, instead of the small snapshot of daily life. Then, chances are, you're trying to keep God number one in your life.

That isn't something you decide once and then forget. Every morning you need to make a choice ... "Who will be number one in my life, God or me?"

Heavenly Father,

So many things in my life are grabbing for my attention, trying to make themselves first place. Help me to see past all of the distractions and maintain my focus on You. I want You to be the number-one priority in my life.

Amen.

Protection

The LORD will go before you,
And the God of Israel will be
your rear guard.
ISAIAH 52:12 NKJV

This is a wise, sane Christian faith:
that a man commit himself, his life,
and his hopes to God, and that God
undertakes the special protection of that man.
GEORGE MACDONALD

He has put his angels
in charge of you to watch
over you wherever you go.
PSALM 91:11 NCV

Placing Your Life into His Hands

The LORD will protect you from all dangers;
he will guard your life.
The LORD will guard you as you come and go,
both now and forever.

PSALM 121:7–8 NCV

You can eat your vegetables, wear your seat belt, always hike with a buddy, even be a black belt in martial arts, but there's only one thing that's guaranteed to offer complete protection anytime, anywhere—putting your life fully in God's hands.

That doesn't mean the laws of physics will no longer apply if you drive faster than the speed limit or that angels will necessarily do physical battle with would-be muggers who happen to come your way. What it does mean is that God will fight for you. He will protect what is most important—your heart and your eternal destiny.

Heavenly Father,

This world is a scary place, but I don't have to be afraid. Thank You for being the sure protection for my life when I place myself fully in Your hands. No matter what comes my way, I know that ultimately I am held safe in Your arms. Nothing can separate me from Your love or my eternal destiny in You.

Amen.

Purity

How to be pure? By steadfast longing
for the one good, that is, God.
MEISTER ECKHART

How can a young person live a pure life?
By obeying your word.
With all my heart I try to obey you.
Don't let me break your commands.
I have taken your words to heart
so I would not sin against you.
PSALM 119:9–11 NCV

There cannot be perfect transformation
without perfect pureness.
JOHN OF THE CROSS

Pleasing Our Companion

Create in me a pure heart, God,
and make my spirit right again.
PSALM 51:10 NCV

Picture Jesus as your constant companion, accompanying you for coffee with your friends, watching a DVD with you late into the night, cheering alongside you in the bleachers at a sporting event, or dropping by a convenience store with you to pick up a magazine. Does knowing that Jesus is right beside you influence the choices you make or the language you use?

If there is any part of your life you'd be embarrassed for Jesus to see or hear, your purity may be in jeopardy. It's easy to forget that God grieves when you go along with the crowd, or your own less-than-pure desires, and do something you know you shouldn't. Dare to do what's right. Choose to keep your heart, and life, pure.

Heavenly Father,

Being pure in this world full of darkness is not easy, but I want to live a life that pleases You. As You walk alongside me each day, I want You to smile as I make right choices. Thank You that You cheer me on as I choose purity over passing pleasures. Help me to dare to do what's right.

Amen.

Purpose

Your talent is God's gift to you.
What you do with it is your gift back to God.

LEO BUSCAGLIA

*As each one has received a gift,
minister it to one another, as good
stewards of the manifold grace of God.*

1 PETER 4:10 NKJV

The real tragedy of life is not
in being limited to one talent,
but in the failure to use the one talent.

EDGAR W. WORK

Here for a Purpose

We all have different gifts, each of which came because of the grace God gave us.
ROMANS 12:6 NCV

If you have discovered your calling in life and are successfully fulfilling it, you are blessed. There are many people today who are still grappling with the questions, "Who am I, and why am I here?"

You may look many places, but you will never find the answers to those questions outside of God. He created you for a purpose and has given you the gifts and talents you need to pursue and fulfill that purpose. Go to Him, humbly and honestly, and ask Him to show you those things He has placed within you and for what purpose He intends them to be used. The revelation of God's gifts in your life may take time, but it's time well spent.

Heavenly Father,

Although I don't know all the details yet, I do believe that You put me here—at this time in history—for a specific purpose. As I look to You for answers, help me to recognize the direction in which You are leading me, as well as the gifts You've placed inside me. I want to develop my talents to the utmost so that they can bless others and glorify You.

Amen.

Relationships

Always be humble, gentle, and patient, accepting each other in love. You are joined together with peace through the Spirit, so make every effort to continue together in this way.

EPHESIANS 4:2–3 NCV

Any deep relationship to another human being requires watchfulness and nourishment; otherwise it is taken from us. And we cannot recapture it. This is a form of having and not having that is the root of innumerable tragedies.

PAUL TILLICH

Jesus said, "Love each other. You must love each other as I have loved you."

JOHN 13:34 NCV

Loving Others Well

Now that you have made your souls pure
by obeying the truth, you can have true love
for your Christian brothers and sisters.
So love each other deeply with all your heart.

1 PETER 1:22 NCV

Want to know what love looks like? Look at God. Consider His sacrifice, His patience, His comfort, His faithfulness, His generosity. God's creativity in expressing love is so great that it's almost incomprehensible.

Consider how your love stands up next to His. Don't get discouraged. You're not God. At times, your love still falters and fails. But, God's love is at work in your life. He's helping you love others in the same wonderful way He so deeply loves you.

Let God's creative compassion inspire you to love others well. Ask His help in knowing the best way to express your love so that it meets needs, builds relationships, and warms hearts. Then, take a moment to sit back and enjoy His love for you.

Heavenly Father,

I'm so glad to have You to look to for my example of what true love looks like. I want to show that same kind of love to others more and more. Thank You that You've promised to help my love increase, as I reach out to share Your love with others.

Amen.

Relationship with God

God's infinitude places him so far above our knowing that a lifetime spent in cultivating the knowledge of him leaves as much yet to learn as if we had never begun.

A. W. TOZER

Jesus said, "It is written, 'Man shall not live by bread alone, but by every word that proceeds from the mouth of God.'"

MATTHEW 4:4 NKJV

God is to us like the sky to a small bird, which cannot see its outer limits and cannot reach its distant horizons, but can only lose itself in the greatness and immensity of the blueness.

JOHN POWELL

There's Always More

I think that all things are worth nothing compared with the greatness of knowing Christ Jesus my Lord. ... I want to know Christ and the power that raised him from the dead.

PHILIPPIANS 3:8, 10 NCV

One of the most exciting things about having a relationship with God is that there is always more on the horizon. The life of a believer is a life of expectancy. A. B. Simpson was once asked if he believed in a "second blessing" experience after salvation. "Yes," he replied, "and a third and fourth! God always has more for you."

Just as He provided the children of Israel with fresh manna to eat each morning, God's mercies are new for you each morning as well. Don't dwell in the past. Wait expectantly for the manna God has for you today. You won't be disappointed.

Heavenly Father,

Just when I think I know all about You, You reveal more of Yourself through Your Word and Your ways. You never cease to amaze me! I don't ever want my relationship with You to grow stale, so I won't just settle for what I learned about You yesterday. Instead, I will partake of the heavenly manna of Your Word each and every day.

Amen.

Rest

Jesus said, "Come to Me, all you who labor and are heavy laden, and I will give you rest. Take My yoke upon you and learn from Me, for I am gentle and lowly in heart, and you will find rest for your souls. For My yoke is easy and My burden is light."

MATTHEW 11:28–30 NKJV

Take rest; a field that has rested gives a bountiful crop.

OVID

The eternal God is your refuge,
And underneath are the everlasting arms.

DEUTERONOMY 33:27 NKJV

God Wants You to Rest

The LORD is my shepherd. ...He lets me rest in green pastures.
He leads me to calm water. He gives me new strength.

PSALM 23:1–3 NCV

Imagine carrying a heavy backpack around with you everywhere you go. Now imagine that people are always asking you to carry their backpacks as well. Impossible? You bet. Your back was not designed to carry that kind of load.

When life starts weighing on you like an overstuffed backpack, chances are that you may be carrying more than God intended for you. Take the load to God. Lay it out before Him. Ask Him what to pick back up and what to leave behind. Lean on Him for strength with any especially heavy problems.

Then, rest against God's strong arms. Close your eyes for just a few minutes and enjoy a mini-retreat. God's presence can lighten the heaviest heart.

Heavenly Father,

Jesus said His yoke was light; You never intended for us to carry burdens that are too heavy for us to bear. Thank You for relieving me of the weight of my troubles, as I turn to You. Help me to release more of them into Your loving hands.

Amen.

Satisfaction

Delight yourself also in the LORD,
And He shall give you the desires of your heart.

PSALM 37:4 NKJV

Fulfillment comes as a by-product of our love for God. And that satisfaction is better than we ever imagined. God can make the pieces of this world's puzzle fit together; he helps us view the world from a new perspective.

ERWIN W. LUTZER

The LORD satisfies me with good things
and makes me young again, like the eagle.

PSALM 103:5 NCV

FEEDING YOUR SOUL

Oh, that men would give thanks to the LORD for His goodness,
And for His wonderful works to the children of men!
For He satisfies the longing soul,
And fills the hungry soul with goodness.

PSALM 107:9 NKJV

Think about that feeling of satisfaction you get when you've eaten a good meal of your favorite foods and you wisely choose to stop eating before you go from full to stuffed.

That's how God wants you to feel about life. A job well done, a dream fulfilled, a relationship healed, a confidence in knowing how much God loves you. There are numerous things God can bring your way that satisfy your heart.

God knows every one of your deepest desires. Trying to fill these desires on your own can lead to frustration—or even lead you away from God. But, letting God fill your desires in His way and in His time leads to satisfaction that lasts.

Heavenly Father,

You know what I hunger for—my deepest desires. Thank You for Your promise to satisfy those desires with good things; things that will build me up, not tear me down. Things that will draw us closer and feed the hunger in my soul. Help me entrust my every desire to You.

Amen.

Scripture

When you read God's word
you must constantly
be saying to yourself, "It is
talking to me, and about me."
SØREN KIERKEGAARD

Every word of God is true.
PROVERBS 30:5 NCV

God did not write a book and send it
by messenger to be read at a distance
by unaided minds. He spoke a Book
and lives in His spoken words,
constantly speaking His words and
causing the power of them
to persist across the years.
A. W. TOZER

God's Love Letter

Your words were found, and I ate them,
And Your word was to me the joy
and rejoicing of my heart;
For I am called by Your name,
O LORD God of hosts.
JEREMIAH 15:16 NKJV

The Bible isn't homework. It's not a textbook you have to study or an assignment you need to complete. It's a love letter from Someone who cherishes having a relationship with you that will never end.

So, read the Bible like you do a letter from a close friend. Don't hurry through it. Savor it. See if your Friend has any requests you need to fulfill or advice for you to follow. See if what's said reveals anything new about how your Friend views you, others, or world situations. Then, respond with a love note of your own, written in the words of a heartfelt prayer.

Heavenly Father,

You cared so deeply for me that You sent me a love letter—Your holy Word. It whispers of Your good plans for our future together and shouts of Your unending love for me. Help me to cherish Your words as I would an endearing letter from a loved one—eagerly read and re-read.

Amen.

Security

Security is not the absence
of danger, but the presence of God,
no matter what the danger.
AUTHOR UNKNOWN

The solid foundation
of God stands, having this seal:
"The Lord knows those who are His."
2 TIMOTHY 2:19 NKJV

In God's faithfulness
lies eternal security.
CORRIE TEN BOOM

A Truly Solid Foundation

The work of righteousness will be peace,
And the effect of righteousness, quietness and assurance forever.
My people will dwell in a peaceful habitation,
In secure dwellings, and in quiet resting places.

ISAIAH 32:17–18 NKJV

There are not many things in life that can be considered totally secure and immovable. However, the ground is usually one of them. Yet, all it takes is a shifting fault line to remind you that even the solid foundation beneath your feet is not fully trustworthy.

God has no fault lines. His promises, power, truth, and love are your only true security. When the world around you starts to shake, relationships shift, your health crumbles, or your finances threaten to fall off the deep end, remind yourself of whom you're standing on for support. Rest the full weight of your troubles on the all-powerful God. He's a foundation that will never fail.

Heavenly Father,

It's so comforting to know that You're a solid foundation, that You are completely secure and trustworthy. Thank You that when I build my life on You and Your promises, I know that I'll stand firm, even when trouble comes. With Your help and guidance, nothing can shake me.

Amen.

Speech

Kind words produce their image
on men's souls, and a beautiful image it is.
They smooth, and quiet, and comfort the hearer.

BLAISE PASCAL

When you talk, do not say harmful things,
but say what people need—words that will
help others become stronger.

EPHESIANS 4:29 NCV

Good words are worth much, and cost little.

GEORGE HERBERT

A Good Crop

Jesus said, "The mouth speaks the things that are in the heart. Good people have good things in their hearts, and so they say good things. But evil people have evil in their hearts, so they say evil things."

MATTHEW 12:34–35 NCV

You don't have to be a genius to know an apple tree produces apples. You wouldn't expect it to produce watermelons or kumquats. It only produces fruit in keeping with the kind of tree it is.

Your heart is the same way. It produces words that reflect the "kind" of heart you have. Sure, people can fake it for a while. They can try to sound sweet and sincere when their hearts are really filled with anger or pride. But, eventually that "natural" fruit is going to blossom.

Watching your words begins with examining your own heart. Ask God if you have any negative attitudes that need pruning. With His help, you can consistently give words of love, instead of carelessly tossing rotten verbal apples.

Heavenly Father,

I want what comes out of my mouth, all of my words, to truly reflect a heart of goodness and love. Please show me if there are any bad "seeds"—negative attitudes—in my heart, and prune out those things in my life that could hinder a good, bountiful crop.

Amen.

Strength

When God is our strength,
it is strength indeed; when our
strength is our own, it is only weakness.
SAINT AUGUSTINE OF HIPPO

I can do all things through Christ,
because he gives me strength.
PHILIPPIANS 4:13 NCV

The weaker we feel,
the harder we lean on God.
And the harder we lean,
the stronger we grow.
JONI EARECKSON TADA

Our Spiritual Personal Trainer

The LORD is my strength and my shield;
My heart trusted in Him, and I am helped;
Therefore my heart greatly rejoices,
And with my song I will praise Him.
PSALM 28:7 NKJV

If you want to strengthen your muscles, you work out. You lift weights, increasing your repetitions as time goes by. The same is true for building up your spiritual muscles. As God trusts you with increasingly heavier responsibilities and you choose to rely on Him more and more, you'll be able to stand stronger, longer—no matter what the circumstances.

The next time you feel weak or afraid, don't believe what you feel. Listen to what God has to say. Rely on the knowledge that you've been working out with your very own Personal Trainer. God knows just the right exercises to help turn your weaknesses into strengths.

Heavenly Father,

I know that there are areas in my life that are weak, areas that need to be made stronger. Thank You for Your promise that where I am weak, You'll help me to be strong, as I rely on You for my spiritual personal training. Help me to build up the muscles of my spirit, Father.

Amen.

Success

To do what God says to do, when
He says to do it—this is success.
MERIWETHER WILLIAMS

Do not forget my teaching,
but keep my commands in mind.
Then you will live a long time,
and your life will be successful.
PROVERBS 3:1–2 NCV

Success is a journey, not a destination.
BEN SWEETLAND

True Success

Always remember what is written in the Book of the Teachings.
Study it day and night to be sure to obey everything that is written there.
If you do this, you will be wise and successful in everything.
JOSHUA 1:8 NCV

Personal success cannot be measured by the make of your car, the size of your paycheck, or even the recognition you receive for a job well done. True success depends on who you are, not on what you've accomplished.

God created you with a unique potential that only you can fulfill. The more you focus on becoming who God intended you to be, the more successful you'll become—no matter what career path you choose.

Use the gifts that God's given you to the best of your ability. Ask God to guide you in making wise decisions. Seek God's approval more than the approval of those around you. Then, your success is sure.

Heavenly Father,

I know the world's definition of success is often different than Yours. My heart's cry is to be successful in Your eyes. Show me the path You want me to take so that I may live a life of value and fulfillment—to be an example of true, eternal success.

Amen.

Thankfulness

No duty is more urgent than
that of returning thanks.

SAINT AMBROSE

*Let us be thankful, because we have
a kingdom that cannot be shaken.*

HEBREWS 12:28 NCV

Thou has given so much to me. Give me
one thing more—a grateful heart.

GEORGE HERBERT

Thanksgiving Every Day

In everything give thanks; for this is the will of God in Christ Jesus for you.

1 THESSALONIANS 5:18 NKJV

You don't need a turkey to celebrate Thanksgiving. All you need is a reason. God has given you more reasons to be thankful than He's created stars in the sky. So, why wait?

Start with what you see ... the clothes you're wearing, the food in the fridge, and the beauty of a summer day. Then, think about the people you love and how they've touched your life. Next, consider what God's given you that can't be held in your hands—things like hope, forgiveness, and your future home in heaven. Sit quietly as God brings even more reasons to mind.

Stopping to say thanks will remind you of how big God is and how good your life is, no matter what kind of day you're having.

Heavenly Father,

If the Pilgrims could stop and thank You in the midst of difficult circumstances—disease, even death—how can I not do the same? Each day, You give me so many reasons to be grateful. Remind me daily of Your love and care for me so that I may grow in thankfulness.

Amen.

Thoughts

Our best friends and our worst
enemies are our thoughts.
A thought can do us more good
than a doctor or a banker
or a faithful friend. It can also
do us more harm than a brick.

FRANK CRANE

In your lives you must think
and act like Christ Jesus.

PHILIPPIANS 2:5 NCV

Keep your thoughts right,
for as you think, so are you.

HENRY H. BUCKLEY

Transformed Thinking

Think about the things that are good and worthy of praise. Think about the things that are true and honorable and right and pure and beautiful and respected.

PHILIPPIANS 4:8 NCV

Every action, attitude, and plan for the future begins in one place: Your mind. That's why God cares so much about what's going on in your cranium. What you spend time thinking about determines what you will spend time doing—and ultimately who you will become.

Before you knew God, your thoughts pretty much centered around one thing: You—meeting your own needs, and keeping yourself happy. But, times have changed. So should your thoughts.

Notice where you let your mind wander. If it heads down any road you feel God would prefer you not to go, consciously change directions. If certain activities negatively influence your thoughts, find alternative ways to spend your time. Changing your mind really can change your life.

Heavenly Father,

I want my thoughts to be pleasing to You. Transform my mind, Lord; change me from the inside out. Help me to dwell on positive thoughts that will bring life to me and honor to You. As my mind is renewed, I know my heart will be also.

Amen.

Time

God says, "At the right time I heard your prayers. On the day of salvation I helped you." I tell you that the "right time" is now, and the "day of salvation" is now.

2 CORINTHIANS 6:2 NCV

Time is not a commodity that can be stored for future use. It must be invested hour by hour.

THOMAS EDISON

There is a right time and a right way for everything.

ECCLESIASTES 8:6 NCV

Making Every Minute Count

There is a time for everything,
and everything on earth
has its special season.
ECCLESIASTES 3:1 NCV

You only get one "today." After 1440 minutes, your today becomes a yesterday. No do-overs, no second chances, no turning back the clock. Choosing how you'll spend the time you have is a big responsibility. You can waste it on what is worthless or invest it in what will last throughout eternity. The choice is yours.

God wants you to live life to the fullest. That begins with making wise, premeditated choices about how you'll spend the days ahead. That doesn't mean you need to book every minute on your calendar or that lying on the beach soaking up a little sun is a waste of time. Just be aware of how easily time slips away—and spend it wisely in light of your priorities.

Heavenly Father,

Thank You for my life—every minute of it. You've given me, each morning, a chance to start fresh, to make every day count. Help me to make wise choices with the time You've given me so that I'll please You and feel true contentment at the end of each day.

Amen.

Tough Times

Tough times never last,
but tough people do.
ROBERT HAROLD SCHULLER

Comfort each other and edify one another, just as you also are doing.
1 THESSALONIANS 5:11 NKJV

Christ made no promise that those who followed him in his plan of re-establishing life on its proper basic principles would enjoy a special immunity from pain and sorrow—nor did he himself experience such immunity. He did, however; promise enough joy and courage, enough love and confidence in God to enable those who went his way to do far more than survive.
J. B. PHILLIPS

Our Best Comforter

Praise be to the God and Father of our Lord Jesus Christ.
God is the Father who is full of mercy and all comfort.
He comforts us every time we have trouble, so when others have trouble,
we can comfort them with the same comfort God gives us.
2 CORINTHIANS 1:3–4 NCV

When you are going through tough times, you may wonder why God allows it. Only God knows the reasons. What you can be sure of is that He will be there for you, no matter what circumstance you encounter. His love and comfort are resources that will see you through your trial.

And don't forget that others are watching as you lean on God's comforting arm in the face of heartache and disappointment. Your example may show them where to turn when they encounter difficulties in their own lives. Your sorrow will not be in vain if you are able to lead one other person to the comforting arms of the Good Shepherd.

Heavenly Father,

Sometimes other people can't comfort me the way I need to be comforted. Only You can, Father. Thank You for Your strong arms that wrap tightly around me and hold me tight. Thank You for being the God of all comfort, a safe and secure haven I can run to.

Amen.

Trust

I have held many things in my hands,
and I have lost them all; but whatever I have placed
in God's hands, that I still possess.

CORRIE TEN BOOM

Trust the LORD with all your heart,
and don't depend on your own understanding.

PROVERBS 3:5 NCV

All I have seen teaches me to trust
the Creator for all I have not seen.

RALPH WALDO EMERSON

Checking the Compass

He who heeds the word wisely will find good,
And whoever trusts in the LORD, happy is he.
PROVERBS 16:20 NKJV

What do you do when your heart is tugging you one way, but you know God is telling you to go in exactly the opposite direction? Trust God. The guidelines He has given you in the Bible do not change, no matter what the circumstances. What He says is always true, always right, and always wise.

Your heart, however well intentioned, can be swayed by emotion, by public opinion, even by things like exhaustion or pride. It's not a trustworthy compass when it comes to leading you in the right direction.

When a decision comes down to following your heart or following God, you don't need to ask for directions. There's only one right way to go.

Heavenly Father,

Sometimes it is difficult to discern which way is the right way to go, but I am comforted when I remember that You've got everything under control. Thank You for having a wonderful plan for my life and for guiding me toward it with every step. I know as I rely on Your leading—my spiritual compass—that You'll keep my feet on the right path.

Amen.

Truth

Absolute truth belongs to God alone.

GOTTHOLD EPHRAIM LESSING

The word of the LORD is right,
And all His work is done in truth.

PSALM 33:4 NKJV

I think the most important quality in a person concerned with religion is absolute devotion to truth.

ALBERT SCHWEITZER

TRUE FREEDOM

Jesus said, "If you continue to obey
my teaching, you are truly my followers.
Then you will know the truth, and
the truth will make you free."

JOHN 8:31–32 NCV

The Bible says that fear can make you a captive—and truth can set you free. What truth is it that has this amazing power over fear? The truth that Jesus Christ has conquered sin, death, and the grave. He has mastered every situation that you could possibly face, forgiven every sin you could possibly commit, and given you eternal life.

So why would you choose to stay inside your prison cell? Take hold of the truth. Meditate on it until you see the doors swinging open before you. You are free to go, to live, to thrive, to love, to be loved, to be fulfilled as a person. And that's the truth!

Heavenly Father,

Why would I want to stay a prisoner of my fears when You've already unlocked my cell with Your words of truth? Help me to recognize each and every fear that is holding me captive, then guide me to the truth that will liberate me. Thank You for giving me the boldness to take that first step toward freedom—to run toward You, knowing that Your arms are open.

Amen.

Wealth

The judgments of the LORD are true;
they are completely right.
They are worth more than gold,
even the purest gold.

PSALM 19:9–10 NCV

Gold will be slave or master.

HORACE

Blessed is the man who fears the LORD,
Who delights greatly in His commandments.
His descendants will be mighty on earth;
The generation of the upright will be blessed.
Wealth and riches will be in his house,
And his righteousness endures forever.

PSALM 112:1–3 NKJV

Riches Beyond Compare

Wisdom is worth more than silver;
it brings more profit than gold.
Wisdom is more precious than rubies;
nothing you could want is equal to it.
PROVERBS 3:14–15 NCV

Success at school or at your job may be your ticket to a higher income bracket. But, no matter what your future net worth winds up to be, you're rich. You found true wealth the moment you chose to follow God, instead of your own prideful heart.

Whether you choose to enjoy the abundance of those riches or bury that eternal treasure and continue striving for the kind of wealth you can hold in your hands will determine how much you enjoy life—and God.

Consider the priceless riches you possess—love, joy, peace, and hope, to mention just a few. No amount of money can buy treasures like these. Enjoy what you've been given by nurturing a thankful heart. Then, share the wealth by pointing others to God's true treasure.

Heavenly Father,

I want true wealth—the kind that lasts eternally and isn't dependant upon the whims of the stock market or success in school or at my job. Teach me to value those riches that are truly precious in Your eyes: a kind and gentle spirit, a love for others and for You. Only these things will bring true happiness.

Amen.

Wisdom

Common sense suits itself
to the ways of the world.
Wisdom tries to conform
to the ways of heaven.

JOSEPH JOUBERT

Wisdom begins with
respect for the LORD;
those who obey his orders
have good understanding.

PSALM 111:10 NCV

Men may acquire knowledge,
but wisdom is a gift
direct from God.

BOB JONES

EMBRACING WISDOM

As a tree produces fruit, wisdom gives
life to those who use it, and
everyone who uses it will be happy.
PROVERBS 3:18 NCV

You don't have to be old to be wise. A lot of old people do really stupid things. But then again, so do a lot of young people. Being wise has less to do with age and IQ than with your ability to apply what God has taught you to your everyday life. Application takes thought, prayer, and effort.

But, to apply something, first you have to know it. As you read the Bible, ask God to help you understand what His words meant to the people they were originally written for, then for you individually. (A "life application" or study Bible can help.) Then, put what God teaches you into practice. The more you do, the wiser you—and your actions—will become.

Heavenly Father,

I know there's a difference between being smart—having a lot of head knowledge—and being wise—making right choices. Help me to grow in wisdom each day. As Your Word promises, making wise choices will not only save me from harm, it will also bring me lasting peace.

Amen.

Work

There's no labor a man can do
that's undignified, if he does it right.
BILL COSBY

Enjoy the work you do here on earth.
Whatever work you do, do your best.
ECCLESIASTES 9:9–10 NCV

He who labors diligently
need never despair, for all things are
accomplished by diligence and labor.
MENANDER

Pursuing Excellence

In all the work you are doing,
work the best you can. Work as if you were
doing it for the Lord, not for people.
COLOSSIANS 3:23 NCV

When you look back at the years of school and work experience you have behind you, you can feel proud about everything you've achieved. But, there's so much more for you to accomplish. Don't let the thought of all the work that's ahead discourage you, though. Let it inspire you. Work is more than something you do to pay the bills. It's a way of making a positive impact on the world around you and reflecting God's example of excellence. It's also an opportunity to use the unique combination of gifts and talents God has given you.

It doesn't matter whether you work on Wall Street or at a drive-through window. Put your whole heart into whatever you do. God can use your efforts to do great things.

Heavenly Father,

Thank You that Your Word encourages me to pursue excellence in all I do and that You've promised to help me be that "faithful employee" whom others can depend upon. Thank You for blessing me with Your favor as I work hard, bringing honor to You by being a good witness.

Amen.